RELIGION IN AMERICA

THE BASICS

Religion in America: The Basics is a concise introduction to the historical development of religions in the United States. It is an invitation to explore the complex tapestry of religious beliefs and practices that shaped life in North America from the colonial encounters of the fifteenth century to the culture wars of the twenty-first century. Far from a people unified around a common understanding of Christianity, this book tracks the steady diversification of the American religious landscape and the many religious conflicts that changed American society. At the same time, it explores how Americans from a variety of religious backgrounds worked together to face the challenges of racism, poverty, war, and other social concerns. Because no single survey can ever satisfy the need to know more and think differently, *Religion in America: The Basics* prepares readers to continue studying American religions with their own questions and perspectives in mind.

Michael Pasquier is Associate Professor of Religious Studies at Louisiana State University. His work on the history of religion in America has been supported by the American Academy of Arts and Sciences, the National Endowment for the Humanities, and the National Endowment for the Arts.

THE BASICS

To My Students

RELIGION IN AMERICA

THE BASICS

Michael Pasquier

Routledge
Taylor & Francis Group

LONDON AND NEW YORK

First published 2017
by Routledge
711 Third Avenue, New York, NY 10017

and by Routledge
2 Park Square, Milton Park, Abingdon, Oxon OX14 4RN

Routledge is an imprint of the Taylor & Francis Group, an informa business

© 2017 Michael Pasquier

The right of Michael Pasquier to be identified as author of this work has been asserted by him in accordance with sections 77 and 78 of the Copyright, Designs and Patents Act 1988.

British Library Cataloguing in Publication Data
A catalogue record for this book is available from the British Library

Library of Congress Cataloging in Publication Data
Names: Pasquier, Michael, author.
Title: Religion in America : the basics / by Michael Pasquier.
Description: New York : Routledge, 2016. | Series: The basics | Includes bibliographical references and index.
Identifiers: LCCN 2016016729 (print) | LCCN 2016033412 (ebook) | ISBN 9781138805569 (alk. paper) | ISBN 9781315752303
Subjects: LCSH: United States--Religion.
Classification: LCC BL2525 .P355 2017 (print) | LCC BL2525 (ebook) | DDC 200.973--dc23
LC record available at https://lccn.loc.gov/2016016729

ISBN: 978-1-138-80556-9 (hbk)
ISBN: 978-1-138-80557-6 (pbk)
ISBN: 978-1-315-75230-3 (ebk)

Typeset in Bembo
by Taylor & Francis Books

CONTENTS

INTRODUCTION

W. E. B. Du Bois (1868–1963), a sociologist and cultural critic of American life in the late nineteenth and early twentieth centuries, offered incisive and at times controversial commentary on the role of religion in the United States. Well known for his 1903 book *The Souls of Black Folk*, Du Bois made a distinction between the concepts of "church" and "religion." A church, he wrote in his magazine *The Crisis* in 1933, is an organization that regulates the creedal beliefs, worship practices, financial obligations, and ethical goals of a group. He saw churches as human institutions grounded in social reality, complete with all the hopes and frailties that come with any human endeavor. Religion was for Du Bois a theory about the ultimate concerns of humanity and moral questions of right and wrong. Such a theory of religion permitted Du Bois to recognize the plurality of truth claims, the dangers associated with confessional exclusivity, and how the influences of religious beliefs and practices extended well beyond the walls of churches.

The lives of most interest to Du Bois were those of African Americans. In a chapter of *The Souls of Black Folk* entitled "Of the Faith of the Fathers," Du Bois identified African American churches "as the social center of Negro life in the United States." He described the historical development of African American churches in the contexts of both slavery and emancipation, always mediated by the prevalence of national trends in race and politics. And he ended the chapter with a kind of religious proposition of his own, one that challenged African Americans to organize against a society with a past, present, and future steeped in white supremacy. Although always suspicious of religion, Du Bois couldn't help but notice the power of religion to change the world, for better and for worse.

Suffice it to say that Du Bois thought a lot about the American experience of religion. Given the pervasiveness of religion in the United States today, it's likely that many of us have given considerable thought to the same, although from our own personal perspectives and educational backgrounds. Like Du Bois, we all come to the subject of religion in America with certain expectations, prejudices, blind spots, and priorities. We all have our own theories of religion, some of them more or less refined according to professional standards that reflect the academic disciplines of history, sociology, psychology, and anthropology, to name a few. Moreover, we all carry with us some knowledge of American history, usually with an emphasis on the political contours of America's past and a relatively thin understanding of the role of religion in that past.

The goal of this book is to introduce you to the academic study of religion in America and invite you to explore the complex tapestry of religious groups and movements throughout American history. We're going to follow in the footsteps of Du Bois – and many others – by putting religion in conversation with other aspects of American society, including themes like history and memory; colonialism and nationalism; politics and law; race and ethnicity; gender and class; science and technology; and fundamentalism and pluralism. We're going to see how religion works *for* some and *against* others, just as Du Bois so poignantly demonstrated in his many writings on the subject of race and religion. And we're going to end with more questions than answers, for this is but a basic introduction to religion in America. Indeed, the success of this book depends on our ability to extend the investigation of religion in America well beyond these pages we turn in our hands.

APPROACHES TO THE STUDY OF RELIGION

Religion is a modern concept. It is an idea with a history that developed, most scholars would agree, out of the social and cultural disruptions of Renaissance and Reformation Europe. From the fourteenth to the seventeenth century, at a time of unprecedented political transformation and scientific innovation, it became possible for people to differentiate between things religious and things not religious. Such a dualistic understanding of the world was simply not available in such clear terms to ancient and medieval Europeans, to say nothing of people from the continents of North America, South America, Africa, and Asia. Wilfred Cantwell Smith, a scholar of comparative religion, thus distinguished between those "throughout history and throughout the world [who] have been able to *be* religious without the assistance of a special term," and those who "mentally mak[e] religion into a thing, gradually coming to conceive it as an objective systematic entity." Scholars usually describe this dualistic understanding of the world in terms of "religion" and "secularism." Put simply, the tension between secular and religious worldviews is one of the things that makes us modern.

Our study of religion in America begins at this critical juncture in early modern history, at which point we see the peoples of Europe, Africa, and Native America encountering and transforming one another in dramatic and sometimes destructive ways. Wilfred Cantwell Smith's critical historical approach to the concept of religion sets us on a course to discover how attitudes toward religion changed throughout American history. His historical methodology also challenges us to consider how today's scholars fit within this long history of conceptualizing, and indeed imagining religion in certain ways. "For this reason," the scholar of comparative religion Jonathan Z. Smith wrote, "the student of religion, and most particularly the historian of religion, must be relentlessly self-conscious" of how and why we define religion. In order for us to take a self-conscious approach to the study of religion, we must have some knowledge of the historical development of the modern idea of religion.

Emile Durkheim (1858–1917) and Max Weber (1864–1920) were pivotal figures in the sociological investigation of religion. In his 1912 book *The Elementary Forms of Religious Life*, Durkheim argued "that religion is an eminently social thing" comprising the basic building blocks of "beliefs and practices which unite [people] into one single moral community." Ten years later, Weber insisted in his book *The Sociology of Religion* that religious thoughts and behaviors were connected to larger economic and material forces in society, which in turn created ethical systems for communities to follow. Taken together, the social theories of Durkheim and Weber have influenced several generations of scholars of religion, some of whom have focused on the study of religion in America. The sociologists Roger Finke and Rodney Stark, in particular, have led the way in describing "the history of American religion" as "the history of human actions and human organizations, not the history of ideas," a conclusion made in the 1990s but with connections back to the revolutionary ideas of Durkheim and Weber.

Of course, ideas and personal experiences do matter to the study of religion, which is why we have psychological theories of religion. Sigmund Freud (1856–1939) and William James (1842–1910), two of the founding architects of the field of psychology, are critical to our understanding of individual religious experiences. Freud, in his 1927 book *The Future of an Illusion*, called religion "the universal obsessional neurosis of humanity," a phrase that reminds us of Karl Marx's claim that religion "is the opiate of the masses." Stemming from his work in psychoanalysis, Freud likened the appeal of religion to emotional, nonrational, and childlike attachments. William James, on the other hand, resisted the inclination of Marx and Freud to reduce religion to a drug or a neurosis, proposing instead a pragmatic theory of religion that accepted the truth and value of religious experiences insofar as they were verified by believers. James's sensitivity to personal aspects of religion was on display in his 1902 book *The Varieties of Religious Experience*, in which he defined religion as "the feelings, acts, and experiences of individual men in their solitude, so far as they apprehend themselves in relation to whatever they may consider the divine."

James, although revolutionary in his thoughts about religious experience, was a product of his time and a reflection of the culture in which he lived. The child of wealthy parents and the brother of the American novelist Henry James (1843–1916), he came of age at Harvard and associated himself with people like Charles Sanders Peirce (1839–1914), later a great philosopher, and Oliver Wendell Holmes (1841–1935), later a Supreme Court justice. His ideas about the suddenness and extraordinary quality of individual religious experiences, according to the scholar Ann Taves, said something about the interconnectedness of Protestant notions of individual agency and psychological notions of the self in America. While James's unique attention to personal forms of religion opened scholars to new avenues of investigation, it also mitigated the importance of social networks that nurtured religious beliefs and practices in the United States and abroad. By situating James's theory of religion in its particular context, Taves did what any good historical anthropologist would do, which is to provide a close reading of how human thoughts and actions shape, and are shaped by, culture.

Many of today's leading scholars take anthropological approaches to the study of religion. Chief among their influences is Clifford Geertz (1926–2006), an American-born and Harvard-trained anthropologist, who described religion as a cultural system of symbols that establish moods and motivations in people; provide them with a general order of the universe; and then cloak those conceptions with a veneer of factuality in ways that seem utterly realistic and true. With this definition of religion in mind, Geertz insisted that the anthropological study of religion requires "an analysis of the system of meanings embodied in the symbols which make up the religion proper" and "the relating of these systems to social-structural and psychological processes." In other words, Geertz was saying that religion does not exist in a vacuum. Rather, religion is akin to art and science in the way in which it is integrated into the social, psychological, and cultural fabric of life. The role of the anthropologist, then, is to provide a "thick description," or interpretive analysis, of particular cultures.

What follows in this book is a careful reflection on the historical development of religion in America, while keeping in mind the social, psychological, and cultural dimensions of change over time and through space. Such a balanced approach to the study of religion in America will not only introduce you to key people, ideas, events, and movements, but also train you to think critically about how we use the term "religion" in light of other factors that influence both the subject of inquiry and those who inquire. Indeed, if we return to our three examples of American theorists of religion – the sociologist W. E. B. Du Bois, the psychologist William James, and the anthropologist Clifford Geertz – we see how the line between the inquired and the inquirer is not always clear in American religious history. All three men were skeptical of religious truth, while at the same time keenly aware of the real-world consequences of religion. Du Bois was especially illuminating on this point. Writing for both black and white audiences in the era of Jim Crow, but no less relevant to audiences today, Du Bois reassures us that we "ought not be puzzled by [our] religious surroundings," as long as we take a critical and respectful approach to the study of religion in America.

STUDYING RELIGION IN AMERICA

The study of religion in America is a multidisciplinary endeavor. It is also a contested topic of considerable debate and revision. Commenting on the diversity of America's "religious heritage" in his 1966 book *A Religious History of America*, Edwin Scott Gaustad noted how "the achievements of man are too rich to permit a sterile cynicism; yet the depravity of man is too evident to justify a soft sentimentalism." It is somewhere in this middle ground between cynicism and sentimentalism that we begin Chapter 2 with a discussion of key trends in the historical interpretation of religion in America. We ask the question: How have scholars and citizens narrated American religious history? We find answers in the development of the academic fields of "church history" in the late nineteenth century and "American religious history" in the late twentieth century. We also locate them in America's "civil religion" and the various ways in which religion has been memorialized in the public sphere. Controversies over such portrayals of religion in America reinforce the point that the legacy of religious entanglement in both scholarly circles and public squares is a live matter for all of us, and therefore one that requires careful historical evaluation.

After a critical analysis of the history and memory of religion in America, the book is structured chronologically from the colonial period to the present. In Chapter 3 – "Religion and Colonialism in Early America, 1400s to 1770s" – we consider the cultural collision of the religious beliefs and practices of Native Americans, Europeans, and Africans, as well as the role of religion in the development of a national identity leading up to the American Revolution. Chapter 4 – "Religion in a New Nation, 1770s to 1860s" – covers the explosive growth and diversification of Christian adherence during the early nineteenth century, due in no small measure to the religious lives of enslaved African Americans and European immigrants. Chapter 5 – "Religion in a Modernizing America, 1860s to 1920s" – picks up with the aftermath of the Civil War and its dramatic impact on the religious organizations of both black and white

Americans. It continues with the ongoing immigration of non-Protestant (Catholic, Jewish, Buddhist, Hindu) people to a modernizing United States, combined with an exploration of how Native Americans reacted to government oppression from religious perspectives. In Chapter 6 – "Religious Diversity in a Globalizing America, 1920s to 2010s" – we track how religion played a role in the Great Depression, World War II, and the Cold War, followed by the impact of religion in the civil rights, feminist, and antiwar movements of the 1960s. Moreover, we see how a new era of immigration contributed to the religious diversity of the American religious landscape, with Buddhists, Hindus, Muslims, and non-European Christians populating much of the United States. And we conclude with a critical reflection on the shape of American religious pluralism in the twenty-first century. By the end, we'll have taken an inclusive approach to the study of religion in America, one that embraces the flexibility and fluidity of religious identities throughout American history.

Some might say that a book of this size on a topic of such complexity can only get us in trouble at the next cocktail party or family dinner. And I'd tend to agree, but only if we fail to recognize that the cumulative effects of these chapters, while not comprehensive, do provide us with ample historical context and theoretical tools for further inquiry into the diversity of religion in America. The net result of reading this book, I hope, is that we will think critically about the concept of religion, recognize the impact of religion in American history, and continue to pursue our own investigations into past and present features of religion in American life. These are not modest goals. But they are achievable if we again consider the path taken by W. E. B. Du Bois, a person who welcomed new ideas and applied them to his critical analysis of the world around him. After all, "There is but one coward on earth," Du Bois wrote in his 1940 autobiography *Dusk of Dawn*, "and that is the coward that dare not know." Of course, we won't know everything there is to know about religion in America after reading this book, but we'll have a running start.

FURTHER READING

Major books that have shaped the academic study of religion include W. E. B. Du Bois, *The Souls of Black Folk* (New York:

THE HISTORY AND MEMORY
OF RELIGION IN AMERICA

Americans like to quote from Alexis de Tocqueville's 1835 book *Democracy in America*. It's seen by some as a "one-stop-shop" for insight into the character of a new and expanding nation that, according to the 25-year-old Frenchman, served as a model of democratic principles for the world to aspire to. Originally commissioned by the French government to study the American prison system, Tocqueville was so "struck" by "the general equality of condition among the people" of the United States that he enlarged the scope of his inquiry to include all of "American society." He was especially interested in knowing how America's democratic experiment might translate to Europe's "Christian nations."

Tocqueville wrote *Democracy in America* with a firm belief in divine providence. He argued that the spread of democracy was a gift from God, and that the United States was the nation that best represented the progress and promise of God's will on earth. Tocqueville began his book with a description of the geography of North America before European colonization, a vast and beautiful landscape that "seemed prepared to be the abode of a great nation yet unborn." As for the native inhabitants of the continent, Tocqueville believed that they were "placed by Providence amid the riches of the New World only to enjoy them for a season; they were there merely to wait till others came." The "others" who came, according to Tocqueville, were Anglo-Saxon colonists from England, the most important being the Pilgrims who settled at Plymouth with "their national characteristics … already completely formed." The Pilgrims were Puritans, a Protestant sect described by Tocqueville as "not merely a religious doctrine, but corresponded in many points with the most absolute democratic and republican theories." Why did the Puritans leave their homeland for North America? According to Tocqueville, it was to "live according to their own opinions and worship God in freedom."

Despite his belief in the power of God to spread democracy, Tocqueville still recognized the "great evils" aimed at people of Native American and African descent. "I believe that the Indian nations of North America are doomed to perish," he wrote, while "oppression has, at one stroke, deprived the descendants of Africans of almost all the privileges of humanity." He foreshadowed the expansion of the United States to the Pacific, and with it the continued displacement of Native Americans and expansion of African slavery. He also anticipated "great calamities" between Northern and Southern states over slavery. But he wrote little about the religious beliefs and practices of Native Americans and Africans, saving such commentary for white "Christians of America." Despite "a multitude of sects" within Protestantism, Tocqueville had "seen no country in which Christianity is clothed with fewer forms, figures, and observances than in the United States, or where it presents more distinct, simple and general notions to the mind." Why so much religious diversity and tranquility in the United States? If you asked Tocqueville, the answer was democracy.

Tocqueville was one of the first people to comment on religion in America for massive audiences in Europe and the United States. But he wasn't the last, as we will see in this chapter on how people have interpreted the history and memory of American religions. On one hand, I share in Tocqueville's recognition that Europeans, Native Americans, and Africans were the main actors who shaped the complex religious entanglements of American history (Asians weren't strongly represented in the United States when Tocqueville wrote his book). But I deviate from Tocqueville's providential and democratic attitude toward the trajectory of that history, as do most of today's scholars. This turn away from exceptionalist narratives of religion in America is a relatively new phenomenon, and one that still provokes the censure of those who view the past through a combination of nationalistic and Christian lenses.

It is not my intention to debate the matter, but simply to demonstrate that the religious past of the United States is a contested topic with a long history of revision. Most of this chapter tracks the evolution of scholarly interpretations of American religious history. It begins in the nineteenth century, an era deeply influenced by a so-called "Protestant moral establishment" which perpetuated the image of America as a Christian nation. And it ends in the present, at a moment when the study of religion in America is a reflection of the modern attention to diversity and pluralism. The last section of the chapter takes a critical look at the so-called "civil religion" of America and the ways in which religion has been memorialized in the public sphere. Controversies over the portrayal of religion reinforce the point that the legacy of religious entanglement in American public life is a live matter, and therefore one that requires careful historical evaluation.

CHURCH HISTORY AND THE PROTESTANT MORAL ESTABLISHMENT

There's no denying the influence of Protestantism in American history. The early nineteenth century, in particular, saw the rise of what the historian David Sehat called the "Protestant moral establishment." Far from a land awash in religious freedom for all, Protestants fused law and politics with religious ideology in ways that diminished the rights of minority religions like Catholicism, Judaism, and Mormonism. The separation of church and state, supposedly enshrined in the First Amendment of the U.S. Constitution, wasn't always upheld during the antebellum period. States provided financial support to select churches; prosecuted citizens for blasphemy and violations of the Sabbath; established laws favoring some religious organizations over others; and required Bible study and Protestant prayer in public schools.

Historians have likened the rise of a Protestant moral establishment to an "evangelical empire." This surge in adherence to evangelical forms of Protestantism occurred during a period known as the Second Great Awakening. Methodist, Baptist, Presbyterian, and Congregationalist churches rode a wave of revivalism through both urban and rural areas of the nascent United States. According to historian Martin Marty, "they set out to attract the allegiance of all the people, to develop a spiritual kingdom, and to shape the nation's ethos, mores, manners, and often its laws." These predominantly white Protestant groups were sometimes inhospitable, if not outright violent toward African Americans and Native Americans, to say nothing of non-Anglo ethnic groups emigrating from European and Asian countries.

It was in the midst of this evangelical awakening that Robert Baird (1798–1863) wrote one of the first historical accounts of religion in the United States. Baird was a Presbyterian minister with a background in the American Bible Society and the American Sunday School Union. He spent much of the 1830s and 1840s in Europe as an agent of the Foreign Evangelical Society. In 1842, while living in Geneva, Switzerland, Baird wrote *Religion in America*, wherein he represented evangelical Protestantism as a wholly progressive movement in American history. Non-Protestant groups threatened that progress. Specifically, Catholics "buried the Truth amid a heap of corruptions of heathenish origin," while Mormons followed "the grossest of all the delusions." For Baird, the past, present, and future of the United States depended on the power of evangelical Protestants to shape civil society into a voluntary assembly of people who took "the Bible as their inspired and sole authoritative guide."

Baird's fusion of Protestant theology and American history remained a common mode of historical analysis during the second half of the nineteenth century. Philip Schaff (1819–93), a Swiss-born and German-trained theologian based in Pennsylvania, took Baird's theological approach to the study of the past to new levels. He wrote *America: A Sketch of Its Political, Social and Religious Character* in 1855. In it, he argued that the separation of church and state caused the diversification of Protestantism into sects, which he considered unbiblical and therefore evil. Yet the alternative – established religion of the kind found in the Catholic nations of Europe – was far worse in his opinion. Like Tocqueville, Schaff believed that "America is, without question, emphatically a land of the future.... It is the favor of Providence ... that [Americans] may faithfully and conscientiously fulfill their mission" to save all of humankind. "Christianity" – and by Christianity, Schaff meant Protestantism – "is the only possible religion for the American people."

Schaff, like many Protestants, connected American history to the events of the Bible. On the question of slavery, Schaff looked to the New Testament for guidance. "The relation of the Gospel to as the largest religious group in the United States, followed by Methodists (4,589,284), Baptists (3,712,468), Presbyterians (1,278,332), and Lutherans (1,231,072). Most African Americans (12 percent of the total population) fell largely into the denominational categories of Baptist and Methodist, further contributing to the heterogeneity of the two largest Protestant sects in the United States. And then there were the dozens of smaller denominations – Episcopalians, Mormons, Quakers, Adventists, Mennonites, and others – that dotted the religious landscape. Protestant historians like Baird and Schaff recognized the growing diversity of religion in the United States. But that didn't mean they liked it. The fifteen million people who immigrated to the United States from 1820 to 1890 threatened to destabilize the Protestant moral establishment, while over 7 million African Americans posed an obstacle to the supremacy of white institutions during the era of Jim Crow. Not surprisingly, these ethnic and racial minorities didn't fit neatly into the white Protestant American narratives of church historians.

This discrepancy in historical accounts of religion in America did not go unnoticed. Catholics and Jews of European descent, as well as African American Protestants, produced alternative narratives that challenged traditional depictions of American church history. Additionally, there were professional historians who replaced theological interpretations of American history with social, economic, and political theories of the past. Yet despite these new approaches, the Protestant orientation of church history remained strong well into the twentieth century, further perpetuating many of the same themes articulated by church historians like Baird and Schaff.

John Gilmary Shea (1824–92), a native of New York who considered joining the priesthood as a young man, was the most prolific American Catholic historian of the nineteenth century. He viewed Catholicism as central to American history. In the preface to his four-volume *History of the Catholic Church in the United States* (1886–92), Shea boasted that "the Catholic Church is the oldest organization in the United States, and the only one that has retained the same life and polity and forms through each succeeding age." Not surprisingly, Christopher Columbus (1451–1506), an Italian-born Catholic who led Spain's first successful expedition to the Americas, was one of Shea's favorite subjects. Much of Shea's work focused on the lives of priests and bishops, as well as the institutional development of dioceses from Baltimore, Maryland, to Santa Fe, New Mexico. But he also wrote books like *The Story of a Great Nation: Or, Our Country's Achievements, Military, Naval, Political, and Civil* (1886), in which he exhibited an eagerness to demonstrate Catholic assimilation into American society.

Shea's success as an historian, combined with the economic and political gains of second- and third-generation Catholic immigrants, led to the foundation of Catholic historical associations in the 1880s and 1890s. These scholarly organizations fostered scholarship that usually fell somewhere between Catholic distinctiveness and American assimilation. Like their Protestant counterparts, Catholic historians viewed America's past through the lens of church history, but from a Catholic perspective that downplayed Protestant claims on the providential promise of the United States.

Jews established historical societies at the end of the nineteenth century that reflected a distinctive Jewish perspective on American history. In 1890, approximately 400,000 Jews from a variety of ethnic and sectarian backgrounds lived in the United States. In 1892, a group of Jewish historians and biblical scholars founded the American Jewish Historical Society. Their official mission was "not *sectarian*, but *American* – to throw an additional ray of light upon the discovery, colonization, and history of our country." Unofficially, their goal was to curtail the rise of anti-Semitism that came with the immigration of Russian and Eastern European Jews to the United States.

Oscar Straus (1850–1926), the first president of the American Jewish Historical Society and the first Jewish member of a U.S. president's cabinet, set his sights on the four-hundredth anniversary of Christopher Columbus's "discovery" of the Americas. He commissioned an historian to write the book *Christopher Columbus and the Participation of the Jews in the Spanish and Portuguese Discoveries* (1894). He also wrote a book on the influence of the Old Testament on the origins of republicanism in the United States, as well as two books on religious liberty: *Roger Williams, the Pioneer of Religious Liberty* (1894) and *The Development of Religious Liberty in the United States* (1896). Why focus so much on religious freedom? Because without it, Jewish citizens of the United States would have suffered even more under the anti-Semitism of America's Protestant moral establishment and growing Catholic population.

The history and mythology of Columbus was also a touchstone for a growing body of professional historians who, not to be outdone by religious historians such as Schaff, Shea, and Straus, tried to avoid making arguments from a particular religious perspective. Arguably the most influential contribution to the direction of American historical studies came in 1893, when the historian Frederick Jackson Turner (1861–1932) delivered a speech entitled "The Significance of the Frontier in American History" to a gathering at the World's Columbian Exposition in Chicago. For Turner, the western frontier, not the Protestant establishment, was most responsible for the Americanization of people from many religious and ethnic backgrounds. Democracy and individualism were the chief products of Turner's concept of the frontier experience.

Turner's "frontier thesis" proved highly influential to many church historians of the twentieth century. Peter Mode applied Protestant notions of providentialism to Turner's argument for American exceptionalism in his 1923 book *The Frontier Spirit in American Christianity*. According to Mode, this "frontier spirit" was most manifest in the Protestant revival movement of the Second Great Awakening and the spread of evangelicalism. William Warren Sweet (1881–1959), founder of what came to be known as the "Chicago School" of thought on religion in America, extended Mode's emphasis on revivalism to his book series *Religion on the American Frontier*, which included denominational histories of Methodists, Baptists, Presbyterians, and Congregationalists. Despite the obvious signs of religious diversity, church historians continued to identify these four Protestant denominations as the heart and soul of American Christianity.

African Americans, most of whom came from Protestant backgrounds, did not fit neatly into the narratives of church historians like Mode and Sweet. Carter Woodson (1875–1950), born in Virginia to former slaves and with a Ph.D. in history from Harvard, filled that void with his 1921 book *The History of the Negro Church*. In addition to tracking the development of African American churches, Woodson joined his friend and sometimes rival W.E.B. Du Bois in reflecting on the past through the lens of race and racism. Unlike Schaff, who highlighted the benefits of slavery to African Americans, Woodson made what was then a bold statement for a professional historian: "The white people of this country are not interested in the real mission of Christ." He criticized white Christians, both in the North and South, for "deceiving the multitude with the doctrine that the Anglo-Saxon [was] superior to other races by divine ordination." Additionally, he identified "the Negro church" as one of the most important social forces in American history, not only for its benefits to African Americans, but also for the way it influenced white Christians.

Despite the work of Woodson and other religious and racial minority scholars, the study of religion in the United States remained dominated by white male Protestant visions throughout much of the twentieth century. In the aftermath of World War II, historians from the Chicago School – men like Winthrop Hudson and Sidney Mead – fashioned consensus histories that highlighted the basic unity of Christian values in America and correlated those values with the highest ideals of American democracy. Hudson urged readers to look to America's Christian past in order to rejuvenate "a robust faith in a living God (judging, correcting, disciplining, guiding, and directing the American people)." Mead made a similar plea, but he did so with a keener eye toward the pluralistic features of religion enmeshed in American culture. The ideas of Paul Tillich (1886–1965), one of the most influential theologians of twentieth-century America, were especially noticeable in Mead's usage of the term "Judeo-Christian" to describe a general religious consensus shared by Americans throughout an otherwise fragmented religious landscape.

THE CHALLENGE OF AMERICAN RELIGIOUS HISTORY

Up to this point in the chapter, only men appear in my discussion of American church history. And if you were to read the books of men like Schaff, Shea, and Straus, you would also notice that almost all of them wrote solely about men. Writing in 1972, the historian Anne Firor Scott made this very point, observing in Mead's book *The Lively Experiment* (1963) that "it would appear that he is simply asserting that American history is the history only of American men," thus leaving out "the female half of the population." Add to the list African Americans, Catholics, Jews, Native Americans, Latinos, Hindus, Buddhists, Muslims, and many other groups, and you've got a much more complete, but also terribly complicated combination of identities that have shaped the religious contours of American life.

It was also in 1972 that the historian Sydney Ahlstrom published *A Religious History of the American People*, effectively tilting the direction of American religious studies away from consensus, providentialist narratives and toward more inclusive renderings of a diverse religious past. He described the cultural upheaval of the 1960s and 1970s as a "post-Protestant era," which led him to pursue "an account [of religion in America that] should above all do justice to the fundamentally pluralistic situation which has been struggling to be born ever since this country was formally dedicated to the proposition that all men are created equal." He called for a "renovation of American church history" and a "paradigm of restoration" that situated non-Protestant and non-white peoples at the heart of American religious history. Ahlstrom's synthetic history was, to say the least, a critical turning point in the study of religion in America. It signaled the reorientation of some scholars away from church history and toward American religious history.

With the intellectual floodgates open, the challenge for scholars was to identify and fill the many gaps in the history of religion in America. Studies ranged from the religious experiences of enslaved African Americans on southern plantations and Catholic immigrants in urban ghettos to the critical reconsideration of previously accepted modes of thinking about the place of Protestantism in American history. The historian Thomas Tweed's 1997 edited volume *Retelling U.S. Religious History* provides us with an indication of how scholars had turned away from their predecessors' quest for a consensus narrative by the end of the twentieth century. Topics in Tweed's book included sexuality, ritual, gender, colonialism, regionalism, and nationalism. By suggesting other motifs and identifying alternative settings for historical analysis, Tweed and his partners channeled Ahlstrom's initial challenge to "look for ways to tell more inclusive stories of America's complex religious past" while minimizing entanglement in nationalistic and theological attitudes toward that past.

The concept of "lived religion" also grew out of efforts to revise the ways scholars thought about American religious history. Like Tweed, David Hall led a group of religious studies scholars to produce the edited volume *Lived Religion in America: Toward a*

History of Practice (1997). Their works highlighted the quotidian, and sometimes unremarkable features, of religious practice. In the words of one of the book's contributors, "lived religion ... points us to religion as it is shaped and experienced in the interplay among venues of everyday experience." These venues could include churches and synagogues and mosques – spaces where we're accustomed to find religion – but they could also be homes and streets and farms – spaces that are usually less regulated by traditional religious authorities. Also critical to the study of "lived religion" was an emphasis on "dissent, subversion, and resistance, rather than harmony, consensus, and social legitimation." Here, scholars were quite intentionally reacting to the previous century's historical approach to the study of religion in America by reclaiming the religious lives of women, non-whites, and non-Protestants.

Today, most scholars would agree that there is a distinction between "American church history" and "American religious history." Although admittedly simplistic, American church history operates from a confessional standpoint that privileges orthodox theology and ecclesiastical authority, while American religious history situates itself within academic disciplines that emphasize religious diversity and popular forms of religious expression. Taking the latter approach comes with the warning that we not disregard the importance of Christian churches to American religious history. After all, religious institutions matter to many Americans, past and present. The challenge of American religious history is to respect the tension between the personal and the institutional, the theological and the practical, the ecclesiastical and the cultural. This book, in many ways, is an exercise in keeping this tension intact.

PUBLIC MEMORY AND CIVIL RELIGION

Of course, scholars aren't the only people producing narratives of religion in America. We might even say that they're some of the last people whose voices are heard in the cacophony of positions on the role of religion in American life. Public memory – or the means by which communities reconstruct the past for popular consumption – is arguably a more powerful and pervasive way in which we learn about religion in America. Museums and monuments, as well as popular media like blogs and YouTube videos, foster an ongoing and sometimes convoluted dialogue about matters as controversial as whether or not America was founded as a Christian nation.

Take, for example, Kirk Cameron (1970-). Once a 1980s television star in the sitcom *Growing Pains*, Cameron has since positioned himself at the center of a growing Christian film industry with strong ties to evangelical Protestantism. In addition to appearing in film adaptations of Tim LeHaye's popular *Left Behind* book series, Cameron also produced the documentary *Monumental: In Search of America's National Treasure* in 2012. In the movie, Cameron leads viewers through a version of American religious history based on the premise that "We've forgotten what made this nation so successful and healthy and prosperous and secure." Who, then, have we forgotten? For Cameron, it's the Pilgrims who founded the colony of Plymouth in 1620 whom we've removed from the annals of American history. According to Cameron, the Pilgrims "understood that throughout history, God has always used a small group of people who were totally committed … and [who] knew that if they kept their covenant with God and with one another [that] God would be faithful [to them]." David Barton (1954-), an amateur Christian revisionist historian with a wide readership among many evangelical Protestants, appears in the film as an "expert" on the history of religion in America. With the aid of flimsy historical evidence, he reinforces Cameron's version of the Christian foundation of the United States while avoiding references to primary sources and secondary scholarship that cast a much more complicated rendering of the nation's religious origins.

The storyline of *Monumental*, while historically inaccurate, nonetheless captures an impulse in many Americans to associate the nation-state with religious beliefs, symbols, and rituals. Just take a walk around the national mall and memorial parks in Washington, D.C. – something that Cameron does in *Monumental* – and you will see temple-like structures and iconic objects devoted to the lives of great American men (and a few women) and American ideals. You will read the inscription, "God who gave us life gave us liberty," on the white marble walls of the Thomas Jefferson Memorial, which was modeled after the Pantheon of Rome. Look above the statue of Abraham Lincoln in his memorial, and you will read, "In this temple as in the hearts of the people for whom he saved the union the memory of Abraham Lincoln is enshrined forever." And situated between the statues of Jefferson and Lincoln is the Martin Luther King, Jr. Memorial, where you can read the Civil Rights leader's quotation from the Book of Amos: "We are determined here in Montgomery to work and fight until justice runs 'down like water, and righteousness like a mighty stream.'"

Why so many obvious references to God? Isn't the United States government supposed to avoid entanglement in religious matters? To answer these questions, some scholars have used the phrase "civil religion" to describe expressions of nationalism that bear a strong resemblance to those of religious systems. Writing in 1967, the sociologist Robert Bellah (1927–2013) claimed that "the separation of church and state has not denied the political realm a religious dimension." On the contrary, he noticed "a heritage of moral and religious experience" in American public life that often promotes the biblical archetypes of "Exodus, Chosen People, Promised Land, New Jerusalem, and Sacrificial Death and Rebirth." The recurrence of these themes, according to Bellah, are especially pronounced in presidential inaugural addresses, references to the Founding Fathers, documents like the Declaration of Independence and the Constitution, and on national holidays like Memorial Day and Veterans Day.

In her 1981 survey of American religious history, Catherine Albanese distinguished between the "manyness of religions" and the "oneness of religion" in America. The manyness of religions refers to religious pluralism and the diversity of distinct religions that have made a home in the United States. The oneness of religion refers to the religious unity of Americans around a public mainstream. Albanese's three-part conception of the oneness of religion elaborates upon Bellah's notion of civil religion (a phrase that was actually popularized by Jean Jacques Rousseau (1712–78) in his 1762 book *The Social Contract*). First, according to Albanese, the historical dominance of Protestant denominations produced a form of "public Protestantism" that proved influential even to non-Protestants. Second, "civil religion" is more or less synonymous with religious nationalism that perpetuates an image of the United States as a chosen nation. And third, Americans experience a kind of "cultural religion" throughout their daily lives in the form of popular media.

Obviously, Albanese's historical and sociological description of the oneness of religion in America is different from Cameron's theological and confessional argument for a Christian America. If anything, Albanese helps us understand how public representations of religion inform the stories Americans tell each other about the role of religion in the public sphere and in their private lives. *Monumental*, as a form of public memory, fits rather neatly into Albanese's attention to the historical dominance of Protestantism, the powerful symbolism of religious nationalism, and the pervasiveness of popular culture and media. On the other hand, if we join Albanese in exploring the history of religious diversity in America, then we can see how a film like *Monumental* might attract some viewers while insulting others. It is this "dialectic between the one and the many" that Albanese describes as an "American religious reality" and "a fact of American life."

So, as we have seen, the history and memory of the American religious landscape depend on the stories we tell ourselves and the stories we are told by others. Tocqueville and Cameron, although separated by 170 years, made strikingly similar arguments for America's exceptional position among the world's nation-states in the eyes of a Christian god. Many church historians of the nineteenth and twentieth centuries, although trained in modern historical methods, also viewed America's religious past through theological lenses, with some of their conclusions driven by evangelistic and providential impulses. It wasn't until the second half of the twentieth century that professional historians made a noticeable step outside of confessional boxes and reoriented the study of American religious history in a pluralistic direction. All of this historical wrangling and contested storytelling has led us to the book we are reading now. It goes to show that even a basic survey of religion in America, like this one, comes out of a complex tradition of historical interpretation that is always subject to criticism.

SUMMARY

- There are many ways in which scholars have represented the history of religion in the United States, ranging from confessional arguments for America's Christian origins to evaluations of the religious diversity of American society.

- Protestant historians dominated the field of American church history during the nineteenth century. Their studies tended to blend theological justification with historical analysis, while also focusing on the predominance of white Protestant institutions in American life.

- Alternative narratives of American church history included the perspectives of Roman Catholics, Jews, and African Americans, minority groups that were typically under-represented in white Protestant historical circles.

- During the twentieth century, some scholars started to deviate from confessional interpretations of America's religious past. The causes of this shift included the professionalization of the field of historical studies and the changing religious composition of the American population.

- By the end of the twentieth century, many scholars abandoned the phrase "American church history," choosing instead to use the phrase "American religious history" as a way to provide a more inclusive rendering of America's religious diversity. Historians of American religion placed greater emphasis on people of color, women, non-Protestant groups, and the "lived religion" of all Americans.

- Professionally trained scholars aren't the only people to interpret the history of religion in America. Popular forms of media like film and journalism also contribute to the mass consumption of information about American religious history.

- "American civil religion" refers to the combination of religious symbols and rituals with expressions of American nationalism and identity. Some features of American civil religion appear in the celebration of national holidays, visits to national monuments, and respect for national documents like the Declaration of Independence.

FURTHER READING

For critical reflections on the religious origins of the United States, see David Sehat, *The Myth of American Religious Freedom* (New York: Oxford University Press, 2011); John Fea, *Was America*

Founded as a Christian Nation? A Historical Introduction (Louisville, KY: Westminster John Knox Press, 2011); and Steven Green, *Inventing a Christian America: The Myth of the Religious Founding* (New York: Oxford University Press, 2015). For an overview of historical examinations of "church history," see Henry Bowden's two books, *Church History in the Age of Science: Historiographical Patterns in the United States, 1876–1918* (Chapel Hill: University of North Carolina Press, 1971) and *Church History in an Age of Uncertainty: Historiographical Patterns in the United States, 1906–1990* (Carbondale: Southern Illinois University Press, 1991). For general surveys of American religious history, see Sydney Ahlstrom, *A Religious History of the American People* (New Haven, CT: Yale University Press, 2004); Edwin Gaustad and Leigh Schmidt, *The Religious History of America: The Heart of the American Story from Colonial Times to Today* (New York: HarperOne, 2004); John Corrigan and Winthrop Hudson, *Religion in America*, 8th Edition (London: Routledge, 2010); and Catherine Albanese, *America: Religions and Religion*, 5th Edition (Boston: Wadsworth, 2012). Books that represent recent trends in American religious history include Thomas Tweed, ed., *Retelling U.S. Religious History* (Berkeley: University of California Press, 1997); and David Hall, ed., *Lived Religion in America: Toward a History of Practice* (Princeton, NJ: Princeton University Press, 1997). For works on the concept of "civil religion," see Robert Bellah, "Civil Religion in America," *Daedalus* 96, no. 1 (Winter 1967): 1–21; Peter Gardella, *American Civil Religion: What Americans Hold Sacred* (New York: Oxford University Press, 2013); and "Forum: American Civil Religion Revisited," *Religion and American Culture: A Journal of Interpretation* 4, no. 1 (Winter 1994): 1–23.

3

RELIGION AND COLONIALISM IN EARLY AMERICA, 1400s TO 1770s

When and where does one begin a basic survey of religion in America? As we saw in the previous chapter, there's no one answer to this question. Popular narratives often start with the Pilgrims of Plymouth Rock or the Founding Fathers of the American Revolution. Today, most scholars base the origins of American religious history in the times and places that preceded the European colonization of North America. That's why this chapter opens with the religious worlds of Native Americans and Africans, those who would be most affected by the disruptive consequences of colonialism. We then reflect upon circumstances in Europe that fueled the imperial ambitions of Spain, France, and England to colonize what they conceived as a "New World," a chief factor being the Protestant Reformation. The cultural collision of Native American, African, and European religions in colonial America demonstrates the range of Catholic and Protestant responses to life during the sixteenth and seventeenth centuries. By the eighteenth century, we see how a brand of Protestantism known as evangelicalism surfaced and ultimately permeated the British colonies along the Atlantic coast, in many ways contributing to the gradual formation of a national identity with deep roots in Christianity and continued ties to Native American and African peoples.

NATIVE AMERICAN RELIGIONS

Native Americans played a formative role in the religious history of colonial America. After all, somewhere between 2 million and 10 million Native Americans resided on the continent when

Europeans started arriving in the fifteenth century. In his book *Facing East from Indian Country* (2001), the historian Daniel Richter stressed the need to understand the perspectives of Native Americans before and after they encountered European and African peoples. This isn't a radical idea, and yet so often we resort to telling the story of religion in America from a strictly European viewpoint, facing west from the Atlantic.

The diversity of Native American religions at the dawn of the colonial period was staggering, with over 300 languages spoken among hundreds of distinct groups stretching from coast to coast. That being said, the combination of historical records, ethnographic observations, and archaeological findings allows us to make some general claims about Native American religions at the time of European contact. But before making generalizations, it's important to recognize that Native Americans didn't distinguish religion from other aspects of life. They didn't even have words that resemble our modern definition of religion. Native Americans didn't differentiate between natural and supernatural phenomena. Instead, they were two meaningful aspects of a shared reality. It wasn't until Europeans started interacting with Native Americans that Western theories of religion started to influence indigenous beliefs and practices.

If we apply our modern definition of religion to pre-contact Native Americans, three features stand out. First, most Native Americans developed cosmologies that resembled those of Christian Europe and other societies around the globe. A cosmology is a way of understanding how the world was made and how humans fit in that world. Creation myths are central to cosmologies, which Native Americans shared orally from generation to generation. Second, most Native Americans worshiped an all-powerful god or an assortment of gods. These gods could take human form, but they could also assume other animal attributes and demonstrate both male and female traits. Gods, as well as other supernatural entities, were often associated with good and evil, suffering and death, fertility and harvest, and many other matters of daily concern. And third, most Native Americans believed in something like an afterlife. The burial of human remains was a common practice among many Native American groups, often associated with elaborate ritual ceremonies that readied the dead for the continuation of life in other forms and realms.

These attributes of most Native American religions varied according to geographic location and social structure. For example, at around the time of the origin of Christianity, Hopewell Indians (a complex network of ancient Native American groups concentrated along the rivers of the northeast and midwest) spread what is known as an earth-diver myth, in which a hero goes underwater to retrieve the world's first earth matter and lays the foundation for life. Later Indian groups like the Muskogee, Cherokee, Delaware, and Navajo perpetuated versions of this myth. With such a strong investment in the symbolic power of the subterranean world, Indians of the Hopewell tradition built mounds and other earthworks to bury their honored dead.

Indeed, thousands of mounds dot the landscape of North America today. The last of the great mound-building peoples were the Mississippians. Like the Hopewell tradition, the name "Mississippian" refers to a network of Indian groups with its cradle in the Mississippi Valley and with connections from the Atlantic Ocean to the Rocky Mountains. Mounds served as administrative centers of trade, areas of agricultural and urban development, and zones of religious ceremony. Perhaps the most famous of existing mound complexes is Cahokia, located near modern-day St. Louis, Missouri.

Beginning in the eleventh century, Cahokia was a ritual city covering almost fifteen square kilometers. At its center was a cruciform configuration of plazas and a wooden post buried over three meters into the ground. Mircea Eliade (1907–86), an historian of comparative religion, would have called this an "axis mundi," or the "center of the world," a place that is sacred above all else. By the twelfth century, it is estimated that more than twenty thousand people lived in the vicinity of Cahokia. And even after the mega-village of Cohokia declined in population and importance, its influence remained strong throughout the southeast and midwest, right up to the arrival of Spanish and French explorers in the sixteenth century.

Further west in the present-day areas of Nevada, Utah, Colorado, and New Mexico, the Anasazi emerged in the twelfth century as a resilient agricultural society. Unlike their mound-building neighbors to the east, the Anasazi adapted to the rocky landscape by building villages into cliffs and overhangs. The Spanish would refer to similar structures as *pueblos*. Maize was their primary source of food. In such an arid climate, the Anasazi found it necessary to petition supernatural beings for rain and protection against drought. The ceremonial centers of Anasazi life were known as *kivas*, which were round or rectangular rooms dug into the ground and accessed by way of ladder. The ritual movement of bodies in and out of the subterranean space of a kiva symbolized the mythological emergence of Anasazi ancestors and spirits from the underworld to the land of the living. These ancestors and spirits were known as *katsinas*. Tribal offshoots of the Anasazi included the Hopi, Zuni, Acoma, and Laguna Pueblos, all of whom continued to worship *katsinas* in a variety of ways, including the practices of dressing up as *katsinas* and making *katsina* dolls.

While nowhere near comprehensive, the above examples of pre-contact Native American religions remind us of three things. First, many Indian beliefs and practices resembled those of Europeans, and indeed many other religious traditions outside of Europe. Both Native Americans and Europeans would notice the similarities, which would lead to moments of cultural exchange, both creative and destructive. Second, the natural and supernatural worlds were closely linked in Native American societies, resulting in a more holistic understanding of the place of human beings in the cosmos. And third, Native Americans integrated their beliefs and practices into the fabric of daily life, from hunting and farming to trade and warfare. While religious specialists, such as shamans and medicine men, carried the ceremonial duties of prayer and healing, all men, women, and children participated at some level in the religious life of their respective communities.

AFRICAN RELIGIONS

Historians don't know exactly how many people were enslaved in Africa and transported to the Americas. From the early sixteenth to the mid-nineteenth centuries, our best estimates have somewhere between eleven million to fifteen million Africans experiencing the "middle passage" across the Atlantic Ocean. Out of these totals, around 400,000 African slaves arrived in the colonies of North America. Almost all of them came from tribal areas and kingdoms in West and Central Africa, encompassing a range of ethnic and linguistic groups comparable in diversity to Native America and Europe. Scholars typically distinguish between three forms of religion practiced by enslaved Africans: traditional African religions, Islam, and Christianity. The practice of these religions before and during European colonialism meant that no enslaved African moved to North America as a *tabula rasa* for Christian missionaries to evangelize and convert.

Specific features of traditional African religions depended on where one lived and with whom one affiliated. Many practitioners believed that they resided in a world populated by *orishas* (the Yoruba word for "spirits"), which included the idea of a principal deity with oversight over a plethora of lesser deities associated with particular aspects of everyday life (e.g., hunting, harvesting, childbirth, warfighting). Religious specialists (priests) mediated between humans and spirits through ritual songs, dances, sacrifices, divinations, and the like, sometimes with the aid of materials and objects known as *gris-gris* (fetishes). Healing was also an important component of traditional religions, which combined medicinal substances and ritual practices that were supposed to bring the ailing body of an individual back in concert with the larger social network. When healing didn't work, people died. Many believed that the dead became spirits and continued to interact with the living as spirit ancestors. The handling of the dead demanded the careful attention of religious specialists and laypeople alike, because spirits could both reinforce and destabilize social harmony. The expansion of Islam and Christianity into Africa only added to the range of beliefs and practices that we attribute to traditional African religions.

Islam isn't typically associated with the religious identities of enslaved Africans, and yet some historians have estimated that as many as half of slaves exported to North America were captured in areas of West Africa with deep historical ties to Islam. As early as the ninth century, Berber and Arab traders introduced Islam to sub-Saharan Africa. The Senegal and Gambia River valleys – a major slave supply zone known as Senegambia – were sites of Muslim populations for hundreds of years, including periods of intensified slave trading in the seventeenth and eighteenth centuries. At the same time, warfare between Muslim and non-Muslim polities in the supply zones of Sierra Leone and the Gold Coast also led to the capture and sale of Muslim slaves to European traders. Given these facts, the historian Michael Gomez estimates that approximately 200,000 slaves were likely transported to North America from African regions influenced by Islam.

The practice of Islam in West and Central Africa varied from devout observance to creative combinations of traditional African religions and Islam. Arab-speaking Muslim clerics introduced Islam to royal courts and common people alike, bringing with them Muslim modes of dress, diet, and overall behavior. They also established mosques and *madrasas* (Qur'anic schools) in Muslim sections of villages and towns. Some Muslim traders, while not overt proselytizers, performed daily prayers and recited the Qur'an as they traveled through Africa, which would have gotten the attention of some non-Muslims. Invariably, those who converted to Islam retained aspects of their previous traditional religions, and vice versa. For example, traditional religious practitioners sometimes used Islamic amulets inscribed with Qur'anic texts as gris-gris, while some Muslims prayed to Allah and performed rituals of appeasement for local orishas. It was this kind of syncretic form of Islam that some enslaved Africans carried to the colonies of North America.

Christianity didn't influence the lives of many West and Central Africans until European mariners and missionaries started to arrive in the fifteenth century. In 1491, King Nzinga a Nkuwu (d. 1509) converted to Christianity and made it the official religion of the Central African kingdom of Kongo. Roman Catholic missionaries from Portugal gave the king the baptismal name João and quickly gained influence among the noble class. The translation of Christian doctrines into the local language allowed ordinary people to equate their traditional beliefs and practices with those of Christianity. For example, the Kongo high god Nzambi a Mpungu became more or less synonymous with the Christian god, as did many local deities with Catholic saints. For the next three hundred years, Christianity gained widespread adherence at the same time that a series of civil wars dismantled the kingdom into smaller territories controlled by competing warlords. In one instance, a Kongolese woman named Dona Beatriz Kimpa Vita (d. 1706) claimed that the spirit of St. Anthony possessed her to lead a popular movement to restore the kingdom. Trained as a *nganga marinda* (a medium between the human and spirit worlds), Dona Beatriz promoted a version of Catholicism that fused Kongolese modes of thought with those of

Christianity, in one case claiming in a vision that Jesus was born and baptized in Kongo. A Kongo king captured Dona Beatriz in 1706, after which she was tried and found guilty of heresy by Catholic monks. She was then burned alive.

Roughly 90,000 Africans from Kongo and the surrounding Central African region were enslaved and sent to North America. Over half of them ended up on plantations in the lowlands of Georgia and Carolina, while others went to Louisiana. Kongolese Catholic slaves played a leading role in the Stono slave rebellion of 1739, the largest slave uprising in the British colonies prior to the American Revolution. The goal of the rebels, according to the historian John Thornton, was "to escape slavery in Protestant South Carolina to freedom in Catholic Florida." In a separate instance, an Anglican missionary in South Carolina observed in his parish "a few Negroe Slaves [who] were born and baptized among the Portuguese." Before allowing them to receive communion, the priest required that they renounce "the Errors of the Romish Church." Anecdotes like these also applied to Islam, as was the case when the grandson of a Georgia planter remembered "devout mussulmans, who prayed to Allah … morning, noon and evening." As we will see in other parts of this book, the convergence of African forms of Islam, Christianity, and traditional religions with European and American versions of Christianity would only add to the process of religious syncretism in the United States.

EUROPEAN REFORMATIONS

While those indigenous to North America and Africa developed religious systems, those indigenous to the continent of Europe did the same. The Roman Catholic Church, with its pope in Rome, was the dominant religious tradition of Europe during the Common Era. But within Catholicism, people from a variety of backgrounds both reinforced and challenged the orthodoxy of the Catholic Church. Conflict within the Catholic Church reached a highpoint with the Protestant Reformation of the sixteenth century. Since then, historians have quarreled about the causes and consequences of what the historian Hans Hillerbrand described as "one of the great epochs in the history of Western civilization."

To complicate matters, the Protestant Reformation coincided with the exploration of the Americas by the European powers of Spain, France, England, Portugal, and the Netherlands. The imperial competition to claim the imagined riches of the so-called "New World" meant that the theological arguments and military confrontations of Europe would extend to the greater Atlantic world. Within this multicultural and transcontinental context, we see exchange – the sharing of cultural, social, and economic practices – and change – the inevitable alteration of religious systems for everyone living and dying in colonial America. By understanding the religious reformation of Europe, it is possible to understand how both Protestantism and Catholicism fueled the colonial contest for control of North America.

The seeds of the Reformation were already planted when Cristobal Colon, better known as Christopher Columbus, crossed the Atlantic Ocean and founded a short-lived colony on the Caribbean island of Hispaniola in 1493. The Catholic kingdoms of Europe had been fighting for centuries over political and economic supremacy, leading to periods of warfare and revolution that undermined the unity of the Catholic Church. Far from a society composed of highly educated and theologically sophisticated followers of Catholic orthodoxy, most of the laity and the clergy lived in rural, agricultural areas, although urbanization was on the rise in places like London, Paris, and Amsterdam. Religious observance was not restricted to church attendance and the reception of sacraments. It was in the home and on the land that Catholics reacted to the difficulties of life by making pilgrimages to holy sites, promoting devotions to local saints, celebrating festivals with roots in pagan folklore, relying on magic to appease a providential god in the face of natural and personal disasters, and using astrology to understand the machinations of the heavens.

Out of this world of Christian instability came Martin Luther (1483–1546), a Catholic priest and theologian from Germany who criticized the Catholic Church for abuses of authority. In 1517, Luther publicly posted a list of ninety-five theses on the door of a Catholic church in Wittenberg, Saxony. Chief among his complaints were simony (the buying or selling of church offices), usury (money lending with interest), nepotism, and the sale of indulgences. Originally hand-written in Latin, it didn't take long for allies of Luther to translate the theses into German and print them for a wide audience. Luther continued to write about theological topics that challenged the authority of the Catholic Church, which led to his excommunication by Pope Leo X in 1521. Several of Luther's ideas were especially important to the popularity of Protestantism, including the notions that personal salvation rested on faith alone (*sola fide*) and God's truths were contained in scripture alone (*sola scriptura*).

Luther's ideas took the strongest hold in the Scandinavian and Baltic regions of Europe, although theological and military disputes continued between rival followers of Lutheranism during the sixteenth century. In this period of religious and political upheaval, the theologian and lawyer John Calvin (1509–64) broke away from the Catholic Church and found refuge from persecution in the Reformation bastion of Switzerland. During this time, Calvin criticized the Catholic clergy for abuses of authority. He took exception to the Catholic Church's administration of infant baptism, the sacrament of penance, and the real presence of Jesus in the Eucharist. He agreed with Luther in the common priesthood of believers, eliminating the distinction between the laity and the clergy in the eyes of God. In 1536, Calvin published the first of five editions of the *Institutes of the Christian Religion*, wherein he laid the foundation for theocratic rule in Geneva and the expansion of the Reformed Tradition in Europe and North America. One of Calvin's more controversial ideas was that of predestination, or the belief that it is only by the grace of God that some people are elected for salvation while others are not.

A third reformation movement – Anglicanism – also developed during the sixteenth century. King Henry VIII (1491–1547) of England was a critic of the reformed doctrines of Protestantism, leading the Catholic pope to name Henry a "Defender of the Faith." However, conflict between the English crown and the Catholic pope arose over Henry's request for a marriage annulment. When the pope refused, Henry convinced the English Parliament to pass the Act of Supremacy in 1535, which declared that the king was the "Supreme Head" of the Church of England. Although little changed in the way of Catholic theology and liturgy under Henry's rule, the transmission of authority away from the pope to the crown set the stage for later reform movements in England. Of particular note was the publication of the *Book of Common Prayer* in 1549 and 1552. Like the vernacular writings of Luther, the *Book of Common Prayer* provided literate laypeople with an English translation of prayers and worship services previously written in Latin. And in 1611, King James I (1566–1625) commissioned the translation of the Bible into English, which came to be the official Anglican version of the Old and New Testaments.

Puritans, a growing sect of Calvinist reformers, were especially dissatisfied with the Church of England's retention of Catholic practices. Puritans called for a more radical reformation of Christianity. Queen Elizabeth I (1533–1603), upon her succession to the throne in 1558, worked to find a middle ground between Catholicism and Protestantism in the Church of England, which led to the continued persecution of Puritans. Over time, Puritans achieved some political and religious influence, but not without controversy and sometimes violence. It was out of this context that a small number of Puritans abandoned England and established colonies in North America during the early seventeenth century, where they hoped to develop a more fully reformed church.

Described by historians as the Counter-Reformation, the Catholic Church's efforts to curtail the popularity of Protestantism reached a climax with the Council of Trent (1545–63) and continued through the Thirty Years' War of the mid-1600s. During the Council of Trent, the Catholic Church upheld the fundamental principles of apostolic tradition, the seven sacraments, the veneration of saints, clerical celibacy, monastic vows, and the belief in purgatory, among others. But the Catholic Church also recognized, at least tacitly, that deficiencies in the discipline and training of the clergy were partly to blame for the rise of Protestantism. Overall, the Counter-Reformation made Italy, Spain, Portugal, and, to a lesser extent, France, into Catholic strongholds, although the influence of Protestantism continued to reach every corner of Europe.

Why so much interest in the religious controversies of Reformation Europe? Because it would be Europeans, both Protestants and Catholics, who would bring Christianity to the colonies of North America in the sixteenth, seventeenth, and eighteenth centuries. There they would meet Native Americans. There they would bring Africans, some of whom were already Christian. Once together in this unstable world of cultural collision, no religious belief or practice would be left unchanged. Millions would die from disease and warfare in American colonies, while millions more would arrive by ship from European and African ports. Three imperial powers would claim vast territories of North America – Spain in the south and west, France in the north and midwest, and England in the east, with many contested areas in between. It is to these territories that we now turn, where we will see how the religions of Native Americans, Europeans, and Africans adapted to the circumstances of colonialism.

SPANISH CATHOLICISM AND COLONIZATION

Christopher Columbus' "discovery" of the Americas was an extension of Europe's imperial ambitions in Africa and Asia. The difference, of course, was that Europeans had been living and trading and fighting with Africans and Asians for centuries, while Native Americans represented a previously unknown people from an entirely "New World." Spain and Portugal were quick to invest money and manpower in the colonization of the Americas. In a deal brokered by Pope Alexander VI (1431–1503) in 1493, Portugal would ultimately base its colonial activities on the eastern coast of South America, while Spain would concentrate on the western side of South America, the islands of the Caribbean, and the southern reaches of North America. In a statement made by the pope (known as a papal bull), King Ferdinand (1452–1516) and Queen Isabella (1451–1504) of Spain agreed that "the Catholic faith and the Christian religion be exalted and be everywhere increased and spread, that the health of souls be cared for and that barbarous nations be overthrown and brought to the faith itself." Spaniards would argue over the appropriate way to "Christianize" Native Americans for the next three hundred years.

In the 1500s – a century that saw over 200,000 Spaniards emigrate to the Americas – Spanish Catholicism represented a blend of official and folk expressions of Catholicism that reached the Americas on the heels of the forced conversion and expulsion of Muslims and Jews from Spain. For many Spaniards, to be non-Christian was to be a threat to state security and church authority. Native Americans, like Muslims and Jews, were considered non-believers, and therefore subject to a crusader-like mentality that demanded either conversion or destruction. On the other hand, some Spaniards viewed the Americas as the Garden of Eden, a place free from the corruption and turmoil of Reformation Europe. Native Americans were seen as "noble savages," as innocent and wild creatures with the potential to be tame Christians. In reality, the combination of disease, famine, and warfare led to dramatic reductions in Native American populations, in some areas reaching nearly one hundred percent mortality. It was in this world of incredible human suffering and cultural disruption that Spanish newcomers introduced Catholicism to native inhabitants.

One way to understand the convergence of Native American and European religions is through the thoughts and actions of missionaries. Priests were the official representatives of the Catholic Church in Spanish colonies. They came from a variety of religious orders, including Benedictines, Dominicans, Franciscans, and Jesuits. In addition to serving Spanish colonists, priests saw themselves as missionaries to Native Americans, bearers of the Word of God, and arbiters of salvation. The conversion of Native Americans to Christianity was one of their chief goals. The methods for achieving that goal, however, varied according to the place, time, and circumstances surrounding their interaction.

Some priests took a militant approach to Indian missions. Based on a passage from the Gospel of Luke 14:23 – "compel them to come in" – theologians like Juan Ginés de Sepúlveda (1490–1573) believed that Indians were incapable of freely choosing to become Christian. It was incumbent upon missionaries, therefore, to remove Indians from their traditional lifeways and force them to reside in *reducciones*. In these garrisoned mission towns, missionaries taught indigenous peoples about Catholicism while also controlling basic human activities like childrearing, sex, marriage, eating, and work. This all-encompassing approach to Indian conversion meant that to become Christian also required one to become "civilized" according to European standards. Moreover, missionaries relied upon the *encomienda* system of granting land to Spanish officials, who would then require the native inhabitants of that land to offer tribute in the form of valuable minerals and human labor. Many missionaries supported the *encomienda* system because it gave them access to large groups of effectively enslaved people. Mass baptisms of hundreds of Native Americans at once were not uncommon, oftentimes without the complete comprehension and consent of those receiving the sacrament.

There were those who criticized missionaries for their involvement in the brutality of *reducciones* and the *encomienda* system. Efforts to reform Indian missions required sweeping changes to the entire Spanish colonial enterprise, including the abolition of Indian slavery and the inclusion of Indians in the civil justice process. Bartolomé de las Casas (1484–1566), a Dominican priest who actively participated in the early conquest of Cuba, became the leading voice of reform. In 1542, he sent an account of atrocities against Indians to the king of Spain, later published as *A Short Account of the Destruction of the Indies*. His shocking description of violence contributed to the official abolition of Indian slavery and the gradual dismantling of the *encomienda* system. However, in advocating for the rights of Native Americans, las Casas argued for the transatlantic trade of enslaved Africans in order to satisfy the need for labor in the Spanish colonies. Although he would later retract his support for all forms of enslavement, las Casas was partly responsible for advancing a practice that began in 1501 with the first shipment of African slaves to the Caribbean.

The introduction of Christianity to Native Americans followed the path of Spanish conquest. While not nearly as extensive as the flood of Spaniards to Central and South America, Spain started to establish colonies and missions in the southern region of North America after the expeditions of Juan Ponce de León (1513, 1521) and Hernando de Soto (1539–42). Accounts of these expeditions included vivid examples of Europeans and Native Americans trying to make sense of each other's peculiar religious beliefs and practices. It wasn't until French Huguenots (a Protestant sect) settled in present-day Georgia that Spain funded the first permanent settlement in Florida in 1565. Further west, priests set out from Mexico to establish missions in areas that would come to be known as New Mexico and California. The impetus to journey into the interior of North America wasn't based solely on the conversion of Indians. In 1539, for example, the Franciscan priest Marcos de Niza (1495–1558) traveled all the way to present-day Arizona in search of the rumored Seven Cities of Gold. He didn't find them. And neither did Francisco Vazquez de Coronado (1510–54), even with Niza as his guide. But they did encounter the Pueblo peoples of the southwest.

With financial and military support from the governor of New Mexico, Franciscans established missions among the Pueblo in the late sixteenth century. They presented themselves to the Pueblo in ways that would have confounded Spaniards – as wonder-workers who could control rainfall, healers who could prevent disease, and masters who required complete subjugation to their authority. They modeled themselves after Pueblo shamans, whom they saw as their religious competitors. They also incorporated Pueblo beliefs and practices into their presentation of Christian theology and ritual. For example, they associated the Catholic veneration of the saints with the Pueblo devotion to *katsinas*; the Pueblo prayer stick with the Catholic crucifix; the Pueblo observance of seasonal changes with the Catholic calendar of holy days; and the Pueblo stories of creation and supernatural beings with the Catholic interpretation of biblical passages.

The Pueblo never completely accepted the legitimacy of Catholicism. In concert with military and governing authorities, the Franciscans instituted policies to destroy the sacred sites and objects of Pueblo villages. They also supported the arrest, torture, and execution of Pueblo shamans accused of "sorcery." One of the shamans – a man by the name of Popé – survived the ordeal and spent the next five years organizing a Pueblo revolt against the Spanish regime. Popé convinced his followers that the expulsion of the Spanish from their lands would result in the favor of the Pueblo gods. All told, the Pueblo revolt of 1680 left approximately 400 Spaniards dead, including 21 of 33 Franciscan missionaries. Popé is reported to have ordered the destruction of churches, crosses, and any other physical signs of Catholicism. Unity among the Pueblo, however, was difficult to sustain, resulting in Spain's ultimate reconquest of New Mexico in the 1690s.

The events surrounding the Pueblo revolt of 1680 remind us of the strained relationship between Native Americans and Europeans. Jesuit and Franciscan missionaries spent the eighteenth century extending the chain of Catholic missions north into Arizona, west into California, and east into Texas. Under the leadership of Junípero Serra (1713–84), Franciscans worked closely, and sometimes contentiously, with Spanish officials to establish eighteen Catholic missions from San Diego to San Francisco, California. Serra practiced extreme forms of self-mortification. He wore wire lined shirts, whipped himself to the point of bleeding, poured candle wax on his skin to the point of scarring, and beat his chest with stones to the point of bruising. Indians, forced sometimes at gunpoint, received similar forms of physical torment in the missions. They were whipped for petty misbehavior, shackled for attempting to flee, and even killed if they were seen as a threat to the authority of the Spaniards.

Serra and his fellow Franciscans claimed to have converted upwards of five thousand Indians to Catholicism, a small number when compared to the estimated native population of 300,000 in 1769. By 1821, that number would decline to around 200,000. Disease, famine, and warfare took a tremendous toll on the native inhabitants of California, but so too did life inside the missions. As one missionary observed, they "live well free but as soon as we reduce them to a Christian and community life … they fatten, sicken, and die." Such a startling admission reinforces the point that religious encounters in colonial America had flesh and blood, life and death consequences. The transformative and destructive qualities of colonialism left no one's religious beliefs and practices unchanged.

FRENCH CATHOLICISM AND COLONIZATION

In 1534, a small party of French explorers landed in North America. Under the leadership of Jacques Cartier (1491–1557), the French entered the Gulf of St. Lawrence in search of a northwest passage to Asia. They never got there. Instead, they encountered native residents of the St. Lawrence River valley and quickly realized their error in expecting immediate riches in the "New World." Along the way, they met a group of Iroquois Indians from an area that would come to be known as Quebec. At their first meeting with the Iroquois, the French erected a wooden cross and claimed the territory in the name of the French king. Donnacona (d. 1539), an Iroquois chief, was not impressed with the French symbol of territorial conquest and gesture of Catholic superiority. After several years of diplomacy, Cartier arrested the Iroquois chief and his sons at a ceremony celebrating the feast of the Holy Cross. They were shipped to France, where they all perished before Cartier returned to Canada for the last time in 1541.

The case of Donnacona and Cartier speaks to the convergence of religion and colonialism in New France. In those first years of encounter, we see both the French and the Iroquois trying to understand each other, resulting in a considerable amount of conflict. Writing about Cartier's second voyage, a Frenchman commented that the Iroquois "believe in a god they call *Cudouagny*, and maintain that he often holds intercourse with them and tells them what the weather will be like." The Iroquois also believed, according to the French observer, that "when they die they go to the stars and descend on the horizon like the stars." The French, in turn, told the Iroquois about the Christian god and their belief "that one must receive baptism or perish in hell." What we see in this example of French–Indian exchange are common notions of supernatural beings and an afterlife. But we also notice the haphazardness of early efforts at intercultural understanding, leaving much to be imagined for both natives and newcomers.

It wasn't until the early seventeenth century – over sixty years after Cartier's final expedition and following the most tumultuous years of the Protestant Reformation – that the French established permanent settlements under the leadership of Samuel de Champlain (1574–1635). France's primary reason for developing colonies in Canada was to make money. Sending missionaries to convert the indigenous population was an afterthought. Moreover, the English threatened and at times sacked the fledgling colonies of Acadia and Quebec, further limiting the advancement of Indian missions in New France.

By the 1630s, Jesuit missionaries in Quebec built a Catholic infrastructure that could provide for the religious welfare of French colonists. Nuns of the Order of Saint Ursula – women known as Ursulines – also founded a hospital and a convent school for Quebec's growing female population. With fur trading on the rise, the French established a second colony at Montreal in the 1640s. By 1660, approximately 1000 French men and women lived in Quebec, along with an additional 400 in Montreal. Both towns were crucial staging grounds for Jesuit missionaries on their way to territories controlled by the Huron and the Iroquois.

The *Jesuit Relations*, a series of published correspondences about life in New France, provide us with vivid, and sometimes embellished renderings of missionary encounters with Native Americans. In them, we see how some Jesuits rejected the Spanish model of concentrating potential Indian converts in *reduciones*. Instead, they often left the relative safety of French garrisons for the isolated villages of neighboring native groups. Such an approach required that missionaries learn native languages and customs in order to convey the intricacies of Catholicism to an indigenous population already suspicious of French intentions.

The Jesuit Jean de Brébeuf (1593–1649), with the support of several other missionaries, focused evangelistic efforts on the Huron confederacy, France's closest Indian ally in Canada. Yet despite the moderate openness of Jesuits to syncretism – the merging of seemingly disparate religious beliefs and practices – baptisms of Native Americans were rare and sometimes forced. Deadly European diseases among the Huron also heightened tensions. During the 1630s, a combination of smallpox and influenza killed almost twenty thousand Huron. Neighboring Iroquois groups took advantage of the Huron's vulnerability and disrupted Jesuit missions. Many Huron blamed the Jesuits for their troubles. Some saw the "black robes" (a nickname for Jesuits) as evil shamans, on one occasion leading a group of Huron to desecrate a mission chapel and beat missionaries. The level of Iroquois violence against the Huron and the French reached a highpoint during the 1640s. By the end of the decade, the Huron confederacy was in shambles and eight Jesuits – including Brébeuf – were killed by the Iroquois.

Following the consolidation of French possessions into a royal province in 1663, church and state officials sponsored expeditions throughout the Great Lakes region, the Illinois country, and the lower Mississippi valley. Jacques Marquette (1637–75), a Jesuit missionary, and Louis Joliet (1645–1700), a fur trader, teamed up to explore the interior of North America in 1673. They encountered Illinois Indians at various points along the Mississippi River before turning around near the mouth of the Arkansas River. On several occasions, Marquette and Joliet joined Indian groups in calumet ceremonies, which involved rituals of pipe smoking and gift giving. In 1675, Marquette returned to Illinois country, where he established a mission at the village of Kaskaskia (near present-day Utica, Illinois). According to one of his Jesuit companions, Marquette conducted a Catholic mass in the presence of Kaskaskia Indians and "took possession of that land in the name of Jesus Christ, and gave to that mission the name of the Immaculate Conception of the blessed virgin."

Native American women encountered Catholicism in various ways, depending on where and when one lived in New France. The most well-known Iroquois convert to Catholicism was Kateri Tekakwitha (1656–80). Following her baptism and relocation to the Jesuit mission of Sault St. Louis (located across the St. Lawrence River from Montreal, Quebec), Tekakwitha joined an ascetic group of Christian Iroquois women who renounced sex and marriage for a life of bodily self-discipline through fasting, flagellation, and exposure. A Jesuit priest became fascinated by the young Indian convert, at one point reporting to his superiors that she let off a mysterious glow when she whipped herself. While news of Tekakwitha's holiness only grew after her death in 1680, many more Iroquois converts died without fanfare. In fact, the previous year saw over two hundred Iroquois children and adults die from smallpox and other illnesses. Further south in Illinois country, another Indian convert named Marie Rouensa (d. 1725) planned to live a celibate life similar to that of Tekakwitha, until her father, the chief of the Kaskaskia Illinois Indians, and a Jesuit missionary convinced her to marry a Frenchman. Intermarriage between Indian women and French men was a controversial matter, leading one colonial official to warn people about the "adulteration that such marriages will cause in the whiteness and purity of the blood in the children." And yet Rouensa, like other Illinois women, negotiated the boundary between the perceived "savagery" of Native Americans and "civilization" of Europeans in the lives they led as mothers, wives, and daughters, as well as property owners, businesswomen, and lay religious leaders.

The combination of religious ceremony and territorial conquest happened time and time again in New France. The explorer René-Robert Cavelier Sieur de La Salle (1643–87) provides one such example when he and his party of French, Canadian, and Native American men reached the mouth of the Mississippi River in 1682. Like Cartier before him, he ordered the erection of a wooden cross bearing the name of the king of France, followed by the singing of Catholic hymns, firing of guns, and cries of "Vive le Roi." Assisted by the Recollect priest Zenobia Membre, La Salle promised "to establish the Christian religion" in the region. Two years later, while on a second expedition to the Gulf of Mexico, La Salle was killed by one of his own crew members.

The French established the first permanent settlement in Louisiana in 1699. What made Louisiana unique among the colonies of New France was its strong connection to the Atlantic slave trade. Between 1719 and 1743, twenty-three French ships carrying approximately six thousand enslaved West Africans arrived at the frontier outposts of Mobile and New Orleans, only to be sold and scattered throughout the many plantations and farms dotting the banks of the Mississippi River. By 1732, enslaved Africans accounted for approximately sixty-five percent of the total population (excluding Native Americans) of colonial Louisiana.

Enslaved Africans brought a wide array of religious beliefs and practices to Louisiana. Although archival records are few, we can look to the ethnographic observations of French colonists for some insight into how Africans conceived of their place in colonial America. A manager of a plantation near New Orleans described his captives as "very superstitious, and are much attached to their prejudices, and little toys which they call *gris gris*." For the plantation manager, any religion that wasn't Catholicism warranted the title of "superstition." But looking more closely, we see enslaved people looking to their traditional gods and rituals for ways to comprehend the world around them. The retention of African-derived religious beliefs and practices, although difficult to maintain in the context of slavery, provided enslaved people of color in Louisiana with ways to form communities of opposition to white authorities.

Indeed, the violence and suffering of slavery didn't leave Africans completely powerless in colonial Louisiana. In 1731, a group of around a hundred Bambara slaves living on a nearby plantation plotted to attack New Orleans while its French inhabitants were at Catholic mass on Sunday. Another slave conspiracy scare swept through New Orleans in 1732, when colonists expected their slaves to attack them on Christmas Eve. Those attending midnight mass brought guns and ammunition with them. In neither case did widespread violence erupt, although many of the African conspirators were executed for their transgressions. Nonetheless, it's still worth asking, what do these instances of slave insurrection tell us about African religion? For starters, enslaved Africans were watching their European captors. They recognized Christianity as something important to the French and something worth exploiting. They were becoming accustomed to modern notions of religion, which included the idea that there were many different and sometimes competing religions in the world.

Slavery followed French settlements from Louisiana to Illinois throughout the eighteenth century. At the same time, competition between French and British colonies was on the rise. With a French population twenty times smaller than its Anglo neighbors to the east, New France struggled both militarily and economically to acquire new territories and build new alliances with powerful Indian groups. Things came to a head during the Seven Years' War (also known as the French and Indian War), which ended with France yielding its American colonies to the English at the Treaty of Paris in 1763. England quickly instituted anti-Catholic laws and policies against inhabitants of Canada, fueling levels of Protestant–Catholic antagonism that would persist well beyond the colonial period of American history.

ENGLISH PROTESTANTISM AND COLONIZATION

In 1607, 104 English colonists crossed the Atlantic Ocean and landed in an area dominated by the Powhatan Confederacy of Indian tribes. There they established Jamestown, Virginia, the first permanent English settlement in North America. Despite the financial support of the Virginia Company, newcomers experienced severe hardship, disease, supply shortages, and armed conflict with local natives, leaving over eighty percent of the English colonists dead by 1610.

Under pressure from investors back in England, leaders of the Virginia Company redoubled their efforts to stabilize the Jamestown colony. They looked to the Church of England for a solution. In 1612, Thomas Gates (1585–1622), then governor of the colony, instituted the "Lawes Divine, Morall, and Martiall." These included rules against blasphemy (punishable by death), insubordination to ministers (punishable by whipping), skipping church services (punishable by whipping), and murder (punishable by death). They also regulated interaction between English settlers and Indian neighbors, promising "paine of death" to anyone who disrupted trade or attacked Powhatan tribes without the authorization of colonial officials.

The Powhatan Confederacy of approximately 30 native groups developed a tense relationship with the European newcomers.

They traded goods with the English, but they also fought over land rights and other grievances. Without a formal missionary enterprise of the kind in Spanish and French colonies, the Powhatan remained relatively steadfast in their indigenous religious beliefs and practices for much of the early seventeenth century. They worshipped a panoply of spirits, the most important being Okee, a frightening, punitive spirit with creative and destructive powers. They performed rituals associated with hunting, warfare, eating, harvests, and initiation into adulthood. Shamans, known as *kwiocosuk*, usually led the Powhatan in these rituals, while also serving as healers and the stewards of temples known as *quiocosins*.

It was in this world of Powhatan and English convergences that a girl named Amonute lived. Her nickname was Pocahontas (1595–1617). Much has been written about Pocahontas – there's even an animated Disney film about her – although historians have found it difficult to decipher her personal perspective in light of the sometimes questionable English sources that remain. We know that she was the daughter of a powerful Powhatan chief and that she was around eleven years old when the English settled at Jamestown. If we can believe the accounts of Captain John Smith (1580–1631), Pocahontas served as her father's emissary to the English colony. She married a Powhatan man named Kocoum, only to be kidnapped by the English and put under the charge of an Anglican minister. During her captivity, Pocahontas learned how to speak English and received an education in Christianity. Ultimately, we are told that she converted to Christianity, changed her name to Rebecca after being baptized into the Church of England, and married the tobacco planter John Rolfe (1585–1622) in 1614. They had a child named Thomas. The Virginia Company saw Pocahontas as an opportunity for publicity, so they toured her throughout England and even introduced her to the king and queen. She died in 1617 of an unverified illness in Gravesend, England, where she is still buried today.

Such a quick rundown of Pocahontas' life is misleadingly simplistic. It raises more questions than answers. How did she understand her conversion to Christianity? Did Okee and other Powhatan spirits still exist alongside the Christian god in the mind of Pocahontas? Did she and Rolfe marry out of love, or did their marriage serve as a diplomatic gesture of alliance between the English and the

Powhatan? Did she offer Christian prayers of forgiveness before her death? And did the English question the legitimacy of her Christian conversion when they buried her in an Anglican cemetery a world away from her birthplace? It's these kinds of questions that we must ask of the people who experienced the Anglo-Protestant colonization of North America. We might not have all of the answers, but at least we'll know when to admit our ignorance.

Not long after the death of Pocahontas, another group of English colonists settled in what would come to be known as New England. Yet this time the settlers weren't Anglicans. They were Puritans (also known as Pilgrims) escaping the religious persecution of England and the Netherlands. In 1620, under the leadership of William Bradford (1590–1657) and others, they established the colony of New Plymouth. These early settlers subscribed to a separatist version of Puritanism, which meant that they refused to associate themselves with the Church of England. Instead, they organized themselves around independent congregations nested in the towns and villages of the colony. Although church attendance was mandatory, church membership was restricted to those who demonstrated God's grace through personal conversions and professions of faith. Calvinism informed their theological outlook. They saw God's providential hand in everything. And they looked to the Bible for examples of how to survive and thrive in a land described by Bradford as "devoid of all civil inhabitants, where there are only savage and brutish men" who posed as the antichrist.

Another group of Puritans established the Massachusetts Bay Colony in 1630. John Winthrop (1587–1649), the second governor of the colony, delivered a sermon entitled "A Modell of Christian Charity" that summarized the Puritan understanding of colonization. First, it was God's will that they base their new society on biblical principles of community. "True Christians," he said, "are of one body of Christ." Second, such an organization was only possible "under a due forme of Government both civill and ecclesiasticall." In other words, the wedding of church and state was absolutely necessary. Third, God had commissioned them to create a truly Christian society, one that avoided the Catholic trappings of the Church of England. "We are entered into a Covenant" with God, Winthrop announced. "We have taken out a commission" and God has "ratified this covenant and sealed our commission."

However, such a covenant came with a warning: if they broke their promise, the "Lord will surely breake out in wrathe against us [and] be revenged of such a [sinful] people and make us knowe the price of the breache of such a covenant." Ultimately, Winthrop's goal was for his fellow Puritans to "consider that we shall be as a citty upon a hill" for all the world to see.

Although it is true that Puritans fled England in a quest for religious freedom, it is also true that Puritans didn't promise religious freedom to those who contradicted the religious leaders of the Massachusetts Bay Colony. On the contrary, those who dissented against that which was deemed orthodox Puritanism could face severe punishment. Anne Hutchinson (1591–1643) was one such person. Born in England, Hutchinson and her family followed John Cotton (1584–1652), a prominent Puritan minister, to Boston in 1634. She was especially attracted to Cotton's emphasis on a "covenant of grace" (the belief that grace was a gift of God) and rejection of a "covenant of works" (the belief that humans could merit the grace of God). By extension, she and a small group of sympathizers believed that one could have a direct, personal experience of God's grace without the mediation of Puritan clergymen.

Based on the Calvinist notion of predestination, Hutchinson's belief in a covenant of grace wasn't controversial in and of itself. However, when she started to criticize Puritan leaders for encouraging outward signs of sanctification among their congregations, Winthrop and others accused her of antinomianism (literally meaning "one who is against the law"). In 1637, she was tried in court for "trouble[ing] the peace of the commonwealth and the churches here." Seated before a panel of Puritan clergymen and magistrates, she defended her positions with scriptural recitation and theological sophistication. She even questioned the authority of her accusers, at one point saying, "You have power over my body but the Lord Jesus Christ hath power over my body and soul." In the end, Hutchinson was found to be "a woman not fit for our society" and therefore banished from the colony.

Hutchinson and her family found refuge in the nearby colony of Rhode Island. Founded in 1636, Rhode Island was the creation of Roger Williams (1603–84), a Puritan minister who was also banished from Massachusetts for his dissent against church and state authorities. He bought the land from Narragansett Indians and called it the State of Rhode Island and Providence Plantations. He wanted the colony to be "a shelter for persons distressed of conscience," especially religious dissidents like Quakers, Baptists, and Jews. Freedom of conscience – or what Williams called "soul liberty" – trumped religious conformity and coercion. By extension, Williams believed that a "wall of Separation between the Garden of the Church and the Wilderness of the world" made for a good society. If there was a place where Hutchinson might live out her understanding of Christianity, it was Rhode Island.

Puritans reacted to the diversification of Christianity in the British colonies with a mixture of compromise and suspicion. As early as the 1660s, some Puritan ministers argued that people could be members of Puritan congregations even if they didn't experience a personal conversion. Known as a "halfway covenant," this theological innovation represented a compromise between first-generation Puritans – those who tended to be stricter in their adherence to Winthrop's vision of a "city upon a hill" – and second- and third-generation Puritans – those who were less impressed with the authority of Puritan patriarchs like Winthrop. Generational differences, combined with changing economic opportunities and class discrepancies, meant that residents of New England's growing towns didn't always look to local congregations for moral guidance.

By 1675, over fifty thousand English men and women had immigrated to the colonies of New England. The Native American population, on the other hand, had declined from 140,000 to around ten thousand. Although hardly central to Puritan concerns, the Massachusetts general court passed an "Act for the Propagation of the Gospel amongst the Indians" in 1646. John Eliot (1604–90), a Puritan minister who was involved in the excommunication of Hutchinson, was a leading missionary to Native Americans. He translated the bible into the Massachusett language and published an Indian grammar book during the 1660s. He also organized over a dozen "praying towns," where "praying Indians" lived under theocratic rule in a mission-like setting.

The events of King Philip's War (1674–78) placed praying Indians in a difficult and sometimes deadly position between Native American and English hostilities. Matters came to a head when Plymouth officials executed Wampanoag Indians for assassinating

John Sassamon (1600–75), a Massachusett Indian convert to Christianity. Metacomet (1639–76), also known as King Philip, was the leader of the Indian confederation that waged war against the English confederation of colonies. The English saw the war as the work of the antichrist and a battle between the people of God and the people of Satan. Around three thousand Native Americans died during the conflict, with many others shipped to Bermuda as slaves. Approximately one-tenth of the male English population died.

Mary Rowlandson (1637–1711), with the editorial assistance of the Puritan minister Increase Mather (1639–1723), published an account of her eleven-week captivity by the Wampanoag during King Philip's War. Her narrative included biblical references to God's divine providence and human depravity, as well as insight into the daily lives of her Indian captors. Scholars have noted Rowlandson's captivity narrative for its jeremiad tone. A jeremiad refers to a sermon or other form of lamentation that interprets the trials of a people as punishment for transgressions against God's will on earth. King Philip's War was indeed a trial for English colonists. Like the Old Testament prophet Jeremiah's criticism of the Israelites, Rowlandson and Mather attributed the calamities that befell New England to the Puritan abandonment of their covenant with God. If the Puritans didn't reform their ways, so the jeremiad went, then they would suffer the consequences.

In the aftermath of King Philip's War, King Charles II granted the Englishman William Penn (1644–1718) a charter to establish the colony of Pennsylvania in 1681. Making money was the chief aim of his colonial endeavor. But as a devout Quaker, Penn also saw Pennsylvania as a "holy experiment" based on the principle of religious tolerance. Quakers were accustomed to religious persecution, both in England and in Massachusetts, due to their rejection of baptism, the doctrine of the trinity, the sacraments, and tithes to established churches. Quakers also practiced a form of worship known as quietism, which was a silent, contemplative way for individuals to connect to God in the privacy of their own consciences. The spiritual openness of Quakers extended to the realms of politics and government, inasmuch as laws protected the civil liberties of religious dissenter groups. It was in this environment of economic opportunity and religious freedom that Scotch-Irish Presbyterians, Welsh Quakers, and German Mennonites and

Lutherans settled in Pennsylvania and the neighboring colonies of New Jersey, New York, Maryland, and Delaware.

Puritan New England reached a crescendo of commotion at the end of the seventeenth century. During the summer of 1692, over two hundred residents of Salem, Massachusetts, were accused of witchcraft. A special court was established to hear the cases, many of which included the "spectral evidence" of aggrieved victims visited by the "specters" of the demon possessed. Twenty people were executed for supposedly consorting with the devil. In retrospect, what we see is a society deeply impressed by beliefs in the supernatural and deeply paranoid about demographic shifts in the midst of ongoing warfare between the English, French, and Native Americans. It wasn't until Cotton and Increase Mather – son and father – issued arguments against the legitimacy of "spectral evidence" in witchcraft trials that the governor of Massachusetts suspended further arrests. It also didn't hurt that the governor's wife was also one of those accused of witchcraft.

THE GREAT AWAKENING AND EVANGELICAL PROTESTANTISM

The breakdown of Puritanism during the late seventeenth century ultimately precipitated a reorientation in the way Protestantism developed in the American colonies throughout the eighteenth century. With transatlantic antecedents in Germany, the Netherlands, and the British Isles, a general evangelical movement captured the attention of colonists all along the eastern seaboard. Historians have typically associated the rise of evangelical Protestantism with the "Great Awakening" of the 1730s and 1740s, although there were earlier instances of local awakenings in Dutch Reformed churches of New Jersey and Scotch-Irish Presbyterian churches of Pennsylvania. Some of the key features of this multi-denominational movement included an emotional experience of conversion, or "New Birth;" a heightened regard for the Bible; an emphasis on the sacrifice of the crucified Christ; an interest in spreading the message of the gospel; a more accessible mode of preaching; and a popularization of revivalism.

To be clear, the spread of evangelical Protestantism was not a highly organized, centrally controlled religious movement. What happened in Massachusetts and Connecticutist in the 1740s differed from what happened in North Carolina and Virginia in the 1750s. And what happened in Congregationalist and Anglican churches differed from what happened in Presbyterian and Baptist churches. In addition to regional and denominational trends, we also need to account for the role of other social and cultural factors when considering how African Americans, Native Americans, and women applied the precepts of evangelical Protestantism to their daily lives. With so many moving parts, it can be said that the influence of evangelicalism generated a rise in the diversification of Protestantism in the eighteenth century, while at the same time setting the stage for the later development of what we've already described as a "Protestant moral establishment" in the nineteenth century.

So how and why did all of this change take place during the Great Awakening? We can look first to the development of what some have called a "religion of the heart." Jonathan Edwards (1703–58), a prominent theologian and Congregationalist minister in Connecticut, appealed to both reason and emotion when preaching to members of his church. In his most famous sermon "Sinners in the Hands of an Angry God" (1741), Edwards stressed the Calvinist fear of God's almighty power and the utter depravity of humanity. But in many of his other sermons and writings, Edwards also highlighted the freedom of individuals to cultivate a personal relationship with God. Such relationships took outward form in the pews of his and other Congregationalist churches during the 1740s. It was not uncommon for people to weep and rejoice aloud when contemplating the love of God. Even his wife, Sarah Pierpont Edwards (1710–58), exhibited such signs of exhilaration. On one occasion, while listening to someone recite a hymn, her "soul was drawn so powerfully towards Christ and heaven, that I leaped unconsciously from my chair." The hymn "moved me so exceedingly," she recounted, "and drew me so strongly heavenward, that it seemed as it were to draw my body upwards, and I felt as if I must necessarily ascend thither." She fainted soon thereafter.

Not everyone was pleased with what Edwards called "the present revival of religion in New England." Charles Chauncy (1705–87), also a Congregationalist minister, was one of the most outspoken opponents of the growing popularity of evangelical forms of prayer and worship. In his 1743 tract *Seasonable Thoughts on the State of*

Religion in New England, Chauncy espoused the "Old Light" position against the "enthusiasm" of the times, going so far as to describe Edwards and his "New Light" brand of Protestantism as "a *notorious* error." He looked to "an *enlightened Mind*" instead of "*raised Affections*" as "the Guide of those who call themselves Men." As far as Chauncy was concerned, Edwards and the growing number of like-minded evangelical ministers represented a cadre of "seducers" who foreshadowed the End Times.

The example of Sarah Edwards' expression of piety, while acceptable to some evangelical sensibilities, nonetheless raised concerns among both Old Light and New Light clergymen about the role of women in church leadership. Why? Because, according to the historian Catherine Brekus, "[t]he revivals [of the Great Awakening] marked a decisive break with an earlier tradition of female piety" in which "women were absolutely excluded from holding positions of institutional power in the formal public of the church and the state." Given the evangelical exhortation to follow one's individual conscience and spread the gospel message, many women felt empowered to speak on matters of faith with the same authority as ordained male ministers. Bathsheba Kingsley (d. 1748), for example, was a self-proclaimed visionary and itinerant preacher in Massachusetts who, in 1741, publicly admitted to stealing a horse, leaving her house on the Sabbath without her husband's consent, and proclaiming the gospel in neighboring towns. Her pastor and several other New Light ministers, including Edwards, determined that Kingsley had "gone quite *out* of her place" and acted like a "brawling woman." They scolded her for claiming to be a prophetic visionary and instructed her to stop preaching in public.

New Light Congregationalists weren't the only promoters of a "religion of the heart." A complementary strain of evangelical Protestantism called "methodism" developed in Great Britain during the early eighteenth century and ultimately jumped the Atlantic to the American colonies. While attending Oxford University, the brothers John (1703–91) and Charles (1707–88) Wesley joined other Anglican men in forming a "Holy Club" committed to pious living. The Wesley brothers traveled to Georgia in 1735, where they briefly served as missionaries for the Church of England's Society for the Propagation of the Gospel. The Wesley brothers were especially influenced by Moravianism during and after their time in Georgia.

Moravians subscribed to Arminianism, which, among other things, included the rejection of the Calvinist belief in God's "elect." For John Wesley, salvation required individuals to experience a conversion, followed by a lifetime of cultivating personal holiness through self-control and the willful avoidance of sin. Although John Wesley remained an Anglican priest until his death in 1788, he deviated from his fellow clergyman in the way he encouraged lay itinerant preachers to supervise small prayer groups outside the confines of formal Anglican services.

George Whitefield (1714–70), also an Anglican priest with ties to the "Holy Club" at Oxford University, took Wesley's method of preaching to new heights, especially after he extended his ministry in England to the American colonies in the 1740s. Whitefield's notoriety led contemporaries to nickname him "the Grand Itinerant," and later historians to describe him as America's first major celebrity. Why all the fuss? First, Whitefield was a master orator. He preached anywhere there were listeners, both in the churches of various denominations and at outdoor public spaces. Always the Calvinist, he was known to weep openly when describing his sinfulness in the eyes of God, which, by extension, compelled many in attendance to respond in similarly emotional ways. Second, he was an astute promoter. He published his popular sermons for literate audiences from Nova Scotia to Georgia. He also took advantage of the growing number of newspapers to publicize upcoming revivals, producing massive crowds that left even the religious skeptic Benjamin Franklin (1706–90) in awe. And third, Whitefield managed to synthesize what was previously an assortment of local awakenings into an inter-colonial evangelical movement. The common theological thread running through this movement was the concept of "regeneration," or "New Birth." Based in part on a line in the New Testament's Second Epistle to the Corinthians – "If any man be in Christ, he is a new creature" – Whitefield urged his listeners and readers to "never cease watching, praying, and striving, till he find a real, inward, saving change wrought in his heart, and thereby doth know of a truth, that he dwells in Christ, and Christ in him."

Many preachers imitated Whitefield. Among the imitators, many brought evangelical Protestantism to the southern colonies. It was there that the idea of soul equality – the notion that salvation didn't depend on one's social status or racial category – met the institution of slavery. By 1750, people of African descent out-numbered white inhabitants in South Carolina 39,000 to 25,000, while the number of whites just exceeded that of blacks 129,000 to 101,000 in Virginia. The evangelical concept of rebirth, ritual of baptism by immersion in water, and emotional forms of worship resembled many of the Africa-based religious beliefs and practices that were salient in some slave communities. Although still severely limited by the constraints of a slave regime, the southern awakenings of the 1750s and 1760s set African Americans on a path toward Christianity that previous generations of whites resisted on account of the subversive evangelical message of equality in the eyes of God.

The challenge for historians is to distinguish between the reception of evangelical Protestantism by white and black inhabitants of the southern colonies. Whitefield, initially a critic of slavery, was himself a slaveholder who believed that the religious equality of the races didn't require a dismantling of the white supremacist social structure of colonial America. Still other preachers like the Presbyterian Samuel Davies (1723–61) argued that Christianity had a pacifying effect on the enslaved, which he hoped would alleviate the concerns of Virginia's plantation aristocracy and Anglican establishment over the possibility that Christianity might fuel slave insurrections. Regardless, many people of African descent encountered and embraced features of evangelical Protestantism during the eighteenth century. Writing about the time he heard Whitefield preach in Charleston in 1770, for example, the free black John Marrant (1755–91) described the moment at which the Grand Itinerant seemed to point his finger directly at him and say, "Prepare to meet thy God, O Israel." Marrant woke up on the floor thirty minutes later to a woman pouring water on his face and holding smelling oils to his nose. After the meeting was over, Whitefield met with Marrant and immediately said aloud, "Jesus Christ has got thee at last."

Whitefield died in September of 1770, at a time marked by some of the first overt stirrings of the American Revolution. Around ten thousand people attended his funeral at the Old South Presbyterian meeting house in Newburyport, Massachusetts. The outpouring of public mourning stretched to his homeland in England and throughout the American colonies. While in London, John Wesley preached on the death of Whitefield to many of his admirers, paying special attention to Whitefield's "fundamental doctrines" of "the new birth, and justification by faith." Back in Boston, Phillis Wheatley (1753–84), the slave of a wealthy merchant and the first African American to publish a book, penned a poem in commemoration of Whitefield only a week after having heard him preach. She admired his ability to "Inflame the heart, and captivate the mind." She also called him a "saint" and a "prophet" to both Americans and Africans who "long'd to see *America* excel."

In a way, Wheatley's elegy to Whitefield highlights the relationship between the rise of evangelical Protestantism, the Christianization of enslaved people of African descent, and the development of an American national identity. The evangelical movement of the eighteenth century created a space for Protestant dissenters like Methodists and Baptists to challenge the authority of established churches like Congregationalism and Anglicanism, resulting in the multiplication of churches and the deeper penetration of Protestantism into the fabric of colonial life. People of African descent participated in this movement, sometimes freely and at other times coerced, leaving remnants of African religious beliefs and practices to later enslaved generations. At the same time, with so many people affected by the evangelical movement's messages of personal salvation and collective revitalization, the awakenings of the eighteenth century cultivated a common American identity that linked people from colony to colony like never before.

SUMMARY

- The study of American religions requires an understanding of religion in Europe, Africa, and North America before and during the colonization of the Americas, because the religious beliefs and practices indigenous to these continents converged in later Spanish, French, and English colonies.
- The Protestant Reformation of the sixteenth century coincided with the European colonization of North America. As a result, conflicts between Roman Catholicism and Protestantism fueled many of the imperial ambitions of Spain, France, and England.
- The colonial activities of both Spain and France included the extension of Roman Catholicism to North America. Spanish

and French missionaries relied upon the support of colonial officials to convert native peoples, but not without considerable and sometimes violent resistance to their evangelistic practices.

- The importation of Protestantism to the British colonies of North America included a range of Christian sects, including Anglicanism, Puritanism, Quakerism, and other dissenter groups. The evangelization of Native Americans was not a priority for most British colonists, and yet religious exchanges between natives and newcomers were common.

- The Great Awakening was a transatlantic, multi-denominational Christian movement that spread throughout the British colonies during the first half of the eighteenth century. Followers of this movement came to be known as evangelical Protestants, a diverse group of people who nonetheless shared an interest in emotional conversion experiences, biblical authority, the sacrifice of the crucified Christ, the gospel message of evangelization, and popular forms of preaching and revivalism.

FURTHER READING

For insight into Native American religions, see Daniel Richter, *Facing East from Indian Country: A Native History of Early America* (Cambridge, MA: Harvard University Press, 2003); Joel Martin, *The Land Looks after Us: A History of Native American Religion* (New York: Oxford University Press, 2001); and Joel Martin and Mark Nichols, eds., *Native Americans, Christianity, and the Reshaping of the American Religious Landscape* (Chapel Hill: University of North Carolina Press, 2010). For books on religion in Africa, see John Thornton, *The Kongolese Saint Anthony: Dona Beatriz Kimpa Vita and the Antonian Movement, 1684–1706* (New York: Cambridge University Press, 1998); Jason Young, *Rituals of Resistance: African Atlantic Religion in Kongo and the Lowcountry South in the Era of Slavery* (Baton Rouge: Louisiana State University Press, 2007); Michel Gomez, *Black Crescent: The Experience and Legacy of African Muslims in the Americas* (New York: Cambridge University Press, 2005); and Sylvianne Diouf, *Servants of Allah: African Muslims Enslaved in the Americas* (New York: New York University Press, 1998).

For an introduction to the Protestant Reformation, see Hans Hillerbrand, ed., *The Protestant Reformation* (New York: Harper, 1968); and Diarmaid MacCulloch, *The Reformation: A History* (New York: Penguin, 2005). For works on religion in the Spanish colonies of North America, see David Weber, *The Spanish Frontier in North America: The Brief Edition* (New Haven, CT: Yale University Press, 2009); and Jorge Cañizares-Esguerra, *Puritan Conquistadors: Iberianizing the Atlantic, 1550–1700* (Stanford, CA: Stanford University Press, 2006). For works on religion in the French colonies of North America, see Allan Greer, ed., *The Jesuit Relations: Natives and Missionaries in Seventeenth-Century North America* (Boston: Bedford/St. Martin's, 2000); Allan Greer, *Mohawk Saint: Catherine Tekakwitha and the Jesuits* (New York: Oxford University Press, 2006); and Tracy Neal Leavelle, *The Catholic Calumet: Colonial Conversations in French and Indian North America* (Philadelphia: University of Pennsylvania Press, 2011). For works on religion in the British colonies of North America, see Patricia Bonomi, *Under the Cope of Heaven: Religion, Society, and Politics in Colonial America* (New York: Oxford University Press, 2003); David Hall, *Worlds of Wonder, Days of Judgment: Popular Religious Belief in Early New England* (Cambridge, MA: Harvard University Press, 1990); Jon Butler, *Awash in a Sea of Faith: Christianizing the American People* (Cambridge, MA: Harvard University Press, 1992); Catherine Brekus, *Strangers and Pilgrims: Female Preaching in America, 1740–1845* (Chapel Hill: University of North Carolina Press, 1998); Thomas Kidd, *The Great Awakening: The Roots of Evangelical Christianity in Colonial America* (New Haven, CT: Yale University Press, 2007); and Sylvia Frey and Betty Wood, *Come Shouting to Zion: African American Protestantism in the American South and British Caribbean to 1830* (Chapel Hill: University of North Carolina Press, 1998). For some comparative perspective on European colonies in North America, see James Axtell, *The Invasion Within: The Contest of Cultures in Colonial North America* (New York: Oxford University Press, 1986); and J. H. Elliott, *Empires of the Atlantic World: Britain and Spain in America, 1492–1830* (New Haven, CT: Yale University Press, 2007).

4

RELIGION IN A NEW NATION, 1770s TO 1860s

The formation of the United States of America was never a foregone conclusion. And even when it did become a reality, no one could have anticipated the role that religion would play in the new nation. On the heels of the Great Awakening and at a time of political revolution, many American colonists based their opposition to British rule on philosophical principles of the Enlightenment, longstanding hostility toward the Catholic Church, and Protestant concepts of freedom found in scripture. An explosive growth in church affiliation and religious experimentation followed the American Revolution, much of it fueled by a wave of Protestant revivalism during the early nineteenth century that came to be known as the Second Great Awakening. Black and white Americans contributed to the surge in evangelical Protestantism, many of whom were motivated by their Christian faith to fight for the abolition of slavery. Others (especially white southerners) justified the perpetuation of slavery on theological and biblical grounds. These contrasting Christian worldviews clashed in the American Civil War. Concurrently, Roman Catholic and Jewish immigrants from Europe started to populate urban centers in the East and rural frontiers in the West, sparking demographic shifts that inspired nativism and xenophobia in many Protestant Americans. By midcentury, with so much racial and ethnic variation, we see how even the powerful influence of a white Protestant majority couldn't curb the religious diversification of the United States.

FAITH, REASON, AND REVOLUTION

On a cold London day in January of 1649, King Charles I (1600–49) of England mounted a scaffold, exchanged some final words with his executioner and an Anglican bishop, and lost his head. During the preceding twenty-five years, Charles I had managed to alienate his kingdom's growing body of Puritans and Calvinists to the point of civil war. He was a firm believer in the divine right of kings and an advocate for strong Anglican authority. He also married a Catholic princess from France and levied taxes without the consent of parliament. For these and other reasons, many people viewed the king as a tyrannical monarch with a dangerous affinity toward the Catholic Church. Following his beheading, Charles I was buried next to the corpse of Henry VIII, the same man who had instituted the divine right of kings and formed the Church of England almost a hundred years earlier.

Fast-forward to 1750, when a Congregationalist minister named Jonathan Mayhew (1720–66) mounted a pulpit in Boston, Massachusetts, and delivered a sermon commemorating the hundredth anniversary of Charles I's death. He expressed disgust at "the episcopal clergy" of the American colonies for their treatment of Charles I "as a great SAINT and a MARTYR." Rather than a day of fasting and humiliation, as the anniversary of the king's death had become for some, Mayhew took the occasion to reflect upon "the nature of civil government" and the right to reject "subservien[ce] to the lawless pleasure and frenzy of ONE" tyrannical ruler. Given the harsh content and tone of the sermon, it shouldn't come as a surprise that some historians attribute the slogan "no taxation without representation" to Mayhew, a phrase that captured the growing opposition of many American colonists to the English monarchy, parliament, and church in the decades leading up to the American Revolution.

Mayhew was the product of a political heritage rooted in a form of Protestantism that was open to resistance against the consolidation of government power in the hands of a few. But from the perspective of a growing number of American colonists, Anglicanism wasn't the only religious institution that posed a danger to the colonies. There was also the threat of the Catholic Church, more commonly referred to as "Papism" or "Romanism" by its Protestant detractors. Anti-Catholic sentiment had reached new highs during the French and Indian War (1754–63), a conflict that pitted Catholic France against Protestant England. In 1765, Mayhew tapped into an emerging post-war nationalism when he delivered another sermon entitled "Popish Idolatry," in which he denounced Catholicism as a gross form of demon worship and paganism. In response to "our popish tempters," he called for "a defense of our laws, liberties, and civil rights as men, in opposition to the proud claims and encroachments of ecclesiastical persons, who under the pretext of religion, and saving men's souls, would engross all power and property to themselves, and reduce us to the most abject slavery."

In the aftermath of the French and Indian War, the British parliament passed a series of acts that increased taxes in the American colonies. The Stamp Act of 1765, the Townshend Acts of 1767, the Tea Act of 1773, and the Coercive Acts of 1774 caused much consternation among colonists who called themselves "Whigs" or "Republicans." This group of colonists was heavily influenced by John Locke's (1632–1704) *Second Treatise of Government* (1689), which argued for the right to revolt against a government that broke its social contract with the people. With the signing of the Quebec Act in 1774 – a measure that allowed the Catholic Church to remain the established religion of British-controlled Quebec – the Whigs had had enough. Many Protestant clergymen joined the Whigs in opposition to British colonial rule. Some of their sermons took a millennial tone by equating British tyranny with the coming of the anti-Christ in the Book of Revelation. Still others looked to other books of the Bible for reasons to oppose "slavery" and defend "liberty."

Alongside Whig Protestants, a relatively small but influential group of intellectual elites applied the Enlightenment principle of reason to their justification for revolution. Some of the most prominent proponents of Enlightenment rationalism included Thomas Jefferson (1743–1826), Benjamin Franklin (1706–90), James Madison (1751–1836), and George Washington (1732–99), men who were deeply involved in the production of America's founding documents and new government. Sometimes called Deists, they believed in a providential god that created the universe and provided humanity with natural laws. They did not believe in a supernatural god that revealed truth through scripture. These basic Deistic precepts appear in the wording of the Declaration of Independence (1776) and the Constitution (1789). Correspondingly, the lack of overt references to Christianity in these and other founding documents reinforces the importance of Enlightenment thinking to the original justification for the establishment of the United States.

Many anti-Federalists criticized the Constitution for its apparent "godlessness" and its omission of Christian qualifications for office-holders. They also called for an amendment to the Constitution that would guarantee the freedom of conscience in religious matters. Jefferson and Madison took up this issue in the Virginia General Assembly during the 1780s, effectively articulating what would later be ratified in the First Amendment of the Bill of Rights in 1791. The First Amendment is especially important to our investigation into the history of religion in America. It states that "Congress shall make no law respecting an establishment of religion, or prohibiting the free exercise thereof." In other words, the federal government could neither sanction nor fund a particular religious group over and against another. It also couldn't intrude into the religious beliefs and practices of American citizens. That being said, the Constitution did not prohibit states from establishing official religions and privileging certain Protestant denominations. Most state constitutions, with the exception of Virginia's, supported some form of Christianity-in-general or Protestantism-in-particular. It wasn't until 1833 that the last state – Massachusetts – disestablished religion.

DENOMINATIONAL LIFE AND THE SECOND GREAT AWAKENING

It's important not to overstate the religious motivation behind the American Revolution. While it's true that many Americans viewed the events of the 1770s and 1780s through Christian lenses, historians have shown that other social, political, and economic factors played an outsized role in the creation of the new American republic. In the aftermath of the revolution, however, historians have also observed a reinvigoration of religious adherence that catapulted the new nation into the nineteenth century. Competition among denominations facilitated the expansion of Protestantism throughout the nascent United States and its western territories. Although regular church attendance remained low, few Americans could avoid the impact of the competitive marketplace of religious beliefs and practices that came to be known as the Second Great Awakening.

Four Protestant groups – Anglicans, Congregationalists, Presbyterians, and Baptists – dominated the denominational landscape of the American colonies. After the revolution, these groups experienced considerable reorganization. Anglicans, not surprisingly, suffered the greatest loss of legitimacy and adherence in the new republic. By the 1790s, leaders of Anglicanism in the United States had reorganized the denomination into the Protestant Episcopal Church. Congregationalism remained influential in New England, its traditional stronghold, although old rifts between revivalists and anti-revivalists hampered denominational growth. Presbyterianism managed to avoid major internal conflicts, while at the same time positioning itself to take advantage of the western expansion of the United States. Baptists, the smallest of the four denominations at the end of the revolution, proved the most capable of adapting to the changing religious landscape. By 1800, Baptists comprised the largest denomination in the United States, with popularity rising in both the eastern states and the western interior.

A fifth Protestant denomination – Methodism – surged into the American spotlight following the revolution. In 1784, with authorization from the Anglican priest John Wesley in England, a small group of clergymen met in Baltimore, Maryland, to form the Methodist Episcopal Church. Francis Asbury (1745–1816), born in England and son of a gardener, became one of the first two bishops of the new denomination. Known as an authoritarian, Asbury assigned clergymen to "circuits," or geographic areas, that extended deep into the American frontier. "Circuit riders," as they were called, avoided isolating their ministries to a single church or congregation, choosing instead to travel from town to town and homestead to homestead preaching the Methodist message of holiness and sanctification. By 1820, the number of Methodists surpassed even that of Baptists, making the Methodist Episcopal Church the largest denomination in the United States.

Although hardly a unified revival movement, the Second Great Awakening represented a general resurgence of evangelical Protestant commitments to biblical authority, emotional conversion, and missionary fervor. Its influence surged at different times and in different places throughout the first three decades of the nineteenth century. And its reach included white and black, male and female, rich and poor, and urban and rural residents of the United States. The Second Great Awakening can be broken into three general phases.

New England was the site of the first phase. Congregationalist clergymen, especially those in Connecticut, channeled Jonathan Edward's New Light alliance of Calvinism and revivalism to communities throughout the region. Yale College, with the support of its president Timothy Dwight (1752–1817), became the epicenter of this new revivalism. Dwight was an advocate of immediate conversion who believed that humans played an active role in accepting or rejecting salvation. Among the hundreds of students affected by Dwight's preaching, Lyman Beecher (1775–1863) stood out. Ordained a Presbyterian minister in 1799, Beecher championed Protestant voluntarism (the voluntary basis of church membership and theological adherence) and supported organizations devoted to social reforms like temperance and abolitionism. He also railed against the perceived threat of the Catholic Church to religious freedom. With Protestant unity as one of his chief goals, Beecher preached the millennialist message that "the providence of God is calling upon Christians of every denomination, to cease from their limited views, and selfish ends, and to unite in the conflict which is to achieve the subjugation of the world to Christ."

Cooperation between Protestant denominations was also a feature of the second phase of the Second Great Awakening, which took place in the Old Southwestern states of Kentucky, Tennessee, and southern Ohio. Scotch-Irish Presbyterians streamed into this region during the 1780s and 1790s. They were followed by Presbyterian ministers like James McGready (1763–1817), who worked with local Methodist ministers to organize a series of popular revival meetings in Kentucky in 1800. Revivalism reached a highpoint in 1801, when the Presbyterian minister Barton W. Stone (1772–1844) joined Baptist and Methodist preachers in hosting a revival at Cane Ridge, Kentucky. The week-long "camp meeting," as it was called, attracted approximately twenty thousand participants and set a new precedent for religious revivalism in the western frontier. Given the energy and excitement of the event, many participants responded to exhortations for conversion with physical and emotional outbursts. These "exercises," as they were known, included "falling," "rolling," "barking," "laughing," "dancing," and "jerking." In the middle of a sermon, one Methodist minister counted "five hundred ... lying on the ground in the deepest distresses of agony." Over time, the innovative activities of the Cane Ridge camp meeting became regular features of revivalism in the Old Southwest.

The migration of New Englanders to the Old Northwestern states of New York, Ohio, and Michigan marked the third phase of the Second Great Awakening. The rise of evangelical Protestantism in both rural and urban communities was so pervasive that people referred to the region as the "Burned-Over District." The historian Paul Johnson identified the year 1831 as the climax of this third phase, effectively "mark[ing] the acceptance of an activist and millennialist evangelicalism as the faith of the northern middle class." In addition to focusing on the conversion of individual sinners, evangelists also urged Americans to perfect society through reform movements and benevolent societies. Because of the widespread interdenominational support for these voluntary organizations, the revivalism of the "Burned-Over District" contributed to the development of what has variously been described as "the Benevolent Empire" and "the Evangelical United Front."

Historians usually identify Charles Grandison Finney (1792–1875) – a lawyer from upstate New York who experienced a sudden conversion and became a Presbyterian minister – as the most influential revivalist to come out of the Second Great Awakening, surpassing even Lyman Beecher. In a break from the Calvinist position that humans were innately depraved, Finney proposed that "God has made man a moral free agent" who was capable of choosing good over evil. A willful reorientation of self, he went further, could translate into a social reorientation of the world, ultimately resulting in the perfection of one's soul and society before the End Times. Finney's practical approach to conversion also deviated from the Puritan belief that revivalism was the result of divine intercession. He argued, instead, that "A REVIVAL OF RELIGION IS NOT A MIRACLE;" it "is a purely philosophical result of the right use of the constituted means." Finney and his emulators attempted to convert "backslidden Christians" by employing "new measures" like the "anxious bench" (a row of seats where potential converts faced the revival audience) and "protracted meetings" (a revival that could last for weeks). The popularity of Finney's ideas about revivalism, despite some opposition from Beecher and other evangelists, forged what the historian Daniel Walker Howe called "an ecumenical evangelicalism that could unite evangelicals" against the perceived ills of society.

The combined impact of these three phases of the Second Great Awakening brought women to the center of American religious life like never before. Church membership had doubled between 1800 and 1835, and women represented the majority of those now seated in church pews and participating in revivals. Mothers, wives, and sisters encouraged their male family members to join them in conversion, sometimes resulting in great tension within households. They also comprised the bulk of membership in voluntary benevolent associations that advocated against things like the consumption of alcohol, the use of tobacco, the profanation of the Sabbath, and, in some cases, slavery. The efforts of women to reform American society reflected the perfectionist, millennialist, and missionary attitudes that had come to define the so-called "Benevolent Empire" of evangelical Protestantism.

Over one hundred women worked as itinerant preachers during the Second Great Awakening. Women evangelists like Phoebe Palmer (1807–1874) and Harriet Livermore (1788–1868) challenged the longstanding opposition of most Protestant churches to female preaching. In 1835, Palmer organized a Methodist women's prayer meeting in her New York City home. The wife of a devout Methodist physician and the daughter of an English immigrant who was actually converted by John Wesley, Palmer later extended her domestic meetings for the "promotion of holiness" to the public. Her influence within Methodist circles extended to other evangelical groups after she published the book *The Way of Holiness* (1843), spoke to large audiences at interdenominational camp meetings, and led the Methodist Ladies' Home Missionary Society and other benevolent associations. Arguably better known than Phoebe Palmer, Harriet Livermore was the daughter of a Massachusetts congressman and granddaughter of a New Hampshire senator. Given her privileged position, she was invited to preach before the U.S. Congress on four occasions between 1827 and 1844. The self-described "stranger and a pilgrim" implored her distinguished listeners to prepare for "Judgment Day" and "flee the wrath to come." Her apocalyptic message reached beyond Washington, D.C. through her widely read publications, one of which warned of "a day of trouble – of alarm – of tempest – of great heats – and of great frosts – of sore famines – wars – pestilence – noisome beasts – awful delusions! and horrid desolations!" Yet like so many women preachers, the memory of Livermore was ultimately overshadowed by her male counterparts. In 1868, she died in a Pennsylvania almshouse and was buried in an unmarked grave.

SLAVERY, ABOLITIONISM, AND CIVIL WAR

Many African Americans were involved in the growth of Protestant denominations in the new republic. Free blacks in Philadelphia, with a population of approximately twelve thousand, were especially successful at establishing black-led churches associated with a variety of evangelical denominations. But it wasn't until 1816 that members of Bethel Methodist Church created the first independent black denomination, the African Methodist Episcopal (AME) Church, and elected Richard Allen (1760–1831) as its first bishop. Allen was born on a slave plantation in Delaware and experienced a conversion after encountering Methodist itinerant preachers. Even before he purchased his own freedom in 1786, Allen worked with the Methodist Bishop Francis Asbury to evangelize enslaved and free African Americans. Following his move to Philadelphia, he worked for decades with other black church leaders to end slavery and spread the evangelical message of salvation.

The involvement of African Americans in the Second Great Awakening contributed to a growing anti-slavery movement in the United States. Jarena Lee (1783–1855?), a female itinerant evangelist and protégé of Allen, preached to both black and white audiences that slavery was a sin that deserved God's punishment. The publication of *The Life and Religious Experience of Jarena Lee* (1836) was one among many books and pamphlets circulated by African Americans in northern and southern states. From the perspective of many white Americans, the anti-slavery message of preachers like Lee threatened the white supremacist social order of slave states. For example, in 1822, white citizens seized the property of Charleston's AME church after it was believed that the congregation supported

Denmark Vesey's (c. 1767–1822) failed slave rebellion. Vesey, it was rumored, secretly organized a revolt among the church's four thousand members, most of whom were enslaved. Several years later, pro-slavery whites reacted negatively to the publication of David Walker's (1796–1830) *Appeal to the Colored Citizens of the World* (1829). Walker, a Methodist free person of color, argued that God would judge whites for their treatment of slaves. "America is more our country than it is the whites," he wrote to his fellow African Americans, "we have enriched it with our *blood and tears*."

By 1820, twenty percent of African Americans were Methodist. Still other African Americans attended black Baptist and separate black churches in the South. But more commonly, African Americans attended the churches of their masters, where they sat in segregated galleries and listened to scriptural and theological justifications for slavery. White opposition to independent or semi-independent black churches reached a highpoint in 1831, when Nat Turner (1800–31) led a slave rebellion in Virginia that left approximately sixty whites dead. Turner was a literate slave who read the Bible and believed that God directed him to "fight against the Serpent," which he interpreted as white slaveholders. Following his arrest and while awaiting his execution, he was asked whether he still thought he did the right thing, to which he responded, "Was not Christ crucified!" He was later hanged and skinned. Many whites, including the governor of Virginia, blamed the egalitarian and democratic features of evangelicalism for the events of the Turner revolt. White slaveholders and clergymen responded by intensifying their efforts to Christianize enslaved African Americans, but in ways that diminished the Christian message of freedom.

Slave Christianity was different from the Christianity taught by white preachers and masters. For starters, it included a combination of African, Christian, Muslim, and folk beliefs and practices. It also developed outside the strict confines of churches and revivals, in the fields and slave quarters of plantations throughout the South. The life of Omar ibn Said (1770–1864) is a case in point. Said grew up as a Muslim in northwest Africa, only to be captured and enslaved in 1807, the same year that the overseas slave trade was made illegal by the U.S. Congress. He claimed to have converted to Christianity while a slave in North Carolina. But based on evidence from his Arabic writings, Said may have continued to practice aspects of Islam. Still other enslaved African Americans practiced what the white Presbyterian minister Charles Colcock Jones (1804–63) called "heathenish practices," but which came to be known variously as "conjure" or "hoodoo." Practices associated with hoodoo blended Christian and African rituals of healing and harming that allowed enslaved people to access the spirit world. Such practices converged with slave conceptions of Jesus Christ, Moses, and other biblical figures from whom enslaved African Americans could draw inspiration. Slave spirituals like "Steal away to Jesus" and "Go down, Moses" combined the traditions of African and Christian singing. But as the former slave and abolitionist Frederick Douglass (1818–95) wrote, "A keen observer might have detected in our repeated singing of 'O Canaan, sweet Canaan, I am bound for the land of Canaan,' something more than a hope of reaching heaven. We meant to reach the North, and the North was our Canaan."

Some white Americans joined the abolitionist movement to end slavery. William Lloyd Garrison (1805–79) was by far the most well-known abolitionist of the antebellum period. Garrison's radical anti-slavery ideas were informed by his experience working with Quakers, who were some of the earliest opponents of slavery in the United States. He argued that the U.S. Constitution, because of its support for slavery, represented "a covenant with Death and an agreement with Hell." Finney's ideas of perfectionism also informed the abolitionist positions of many white evangelical Protestants. Theodore Dwight Weld (1803–95), himself converted by Finney, was a leading evangelical voice in the abolitionist movement who worked with Finney to make Ohio's Oberlin College into a bastion of radical social reform. Weld married Angelina Grimké (1805–79), herself an anti-slavery and women's rights advocate, and together they coordinated with the American Anti-Slavery Society to publish *American Slavery As It is: Testimony of a Thousand Witnesses* (1839). In it, Grimké testified to the brutality of slavery in her home state of South Carolina, writing that "the sufferings of the slaves are not only innumerable, but they are *indescribable*." But no book was more influential in the anti-slavery movement than Harriet Beecher Stowe's *Uncle Tom's Cabin* (1852). The daughter of Lyman Beecher, Harriet Beecher Stowe (1811–96) observed slavery while living in Cincinnati, a city that bordered the slave state of Kentucky. She viewed slavery as a national sin, ending *Uncle Tom's Cabin* with an indictment of American churches and an apocalyptic warning of "the wrath of Almighty God!"

Many white Protestants, particularly those in the South, justified slavery on biblical and theological grounds. They pointed to an episode in the Book of Genesis wherein God cursed Noah's son Ham and all of his descendants to enslavement. These descendants, so the argument went, were the dark-skinned people of Africa. A second biblical passage commonly referenced was Paul's letter to the Colossians, which states, "Slaves, obey your earthly masters in everything, not only while being watched and in order to please them, but wholeheartedly, fearing the Lord." Internal debates over slavery ensued in every denomination, leading to the establishment of the Methodist Episcopal Church (South) in 1844, the Southern Baptist Convention in 1845, the New Light Presbyterians in 1857, and the Old Light Presbyterians in 1861. The Catholic Church, although it didn't experience a formal schism, did include members on both sides of the slavery issue. As the historian Eugene Genovese stated, white southerners "insist[ed] that slavery conformed to the Word of God and that, therefore, so did the Constitution of the United States, which, while itself not God's Word, was designed to be consistent with it." But this didn't mean that white southerners believed the practice of enslavement was perfect. As the pro-slavery advocate and Presbyterian minister George Armstrong (1813–99) wrote in his book *The Christian Doctrine of Slavery* (1857), "the Church [must] labor to make 'good masters and good slaves,'" and that "the great duty of the South is not emancipation, but improvement."

After South Carolina seceded from the Union in December of 1860 and the first shots of the American Civil War were fired at Fort Sumter in April of 1861, many citizens in the North and South interpreted the warfare of the next four years through religious lenses. The abolitionist Julia Ward Beecher (1819–1910) wrote the song "The Battle Hymn of the Republic" to the tune of another popular song "John Brown's Body," in which she likened the events of the Civil War to the End Times depicted in the Book of Revelation. She also equated the sacrifice of Jesus Christ to that of the Union: "As He died to make men holy, let us die to make men free/While God is marching on." In the South, the Episcopal

Bishop Stephen Elliott (1806–66) defended the establishment of the Confederate States of America on the grounds that "all nations which come into existence … must be born amid the storm of revolution and must win their way to a place in history through the baptism in blood." The Christian image of a blood baptism reinforced the perspective among white southerners that they, too, were dying for a just and righteous cause.

When the war ended in 1865, over 600,000 American military members were dead. Estimates for civilian casualties probably surpassed 50,000. In the words of the landscape architect and social critic Frederick Law Olmsted (1822–1903), the Civil War had produced a "republic of suffering." Just months before the war ended, President Abraham Lincoln (1809–65) used the venue of his second inaugural address to consider the differences between North and South. Not known for his Christian orthodoxy, Lincoln admitted that Americans "both read the same Bible and pray to the same God, and each invokes His aid against the other." He also expressed the belief that slavery offended God and that "every drop of blood drawn with the lash shall be paid by another drawn with the sword." He ended his address with a call for reconciliation: "With malice toward none, with charity for all, with firmness in the right as God gives us to see the right, let us strive to finish the work we are in, to bind up the nation's wounds." Following the inauguration ceremony, Frederick Douglass attended a reception at the White House. Lincoln asked Douglass what he thought of the address. "Mr. Lincoln," he replied, "that was a sacred effort."

RELIGIOUS EXPERIMENTATION AND NEW RELIGIOUS MOVEMENTS

The religious innovations of the Second Great Awakening weren't restricted to white and black manifestations of evangelical Protestantism. There were new religious movements like Unitarianism and Mormonism that represented, according to the historian James Lewis, "radical theological departures from the dominant Christian tradition." Still other communitarian, millennialist, and restorationist movements arose out of the religious ferment of the new American republic that challenged the orthodoxies of the Protestant moral establishment. While it can be said that these new religious movements remained at the fringe of American religious life, they nonetheless demonstrate the incredible versatility and experimentation of religion in the United States.

The Enlightenment emphasis on human reason influenced Christian Americans from Jonathan Edwards to Charles Finney. By the late eighteenth century, some intellectuals in England and New England used this principle to deny the Christian concept of the Trinity, or the idea that God is three persons (Father, Son, Holy Spirit) in one being. They called themselves Unitarians. Joseph Priestly (1733–1804), an English chemist who discovered oxygen, was an early proponent of Unitarianism in post-revolutionary America after his immigration to Pennsylvania in 1794. Liberal-minded Congregationalists were especially attracted to Unitarianism's suspicion of strict Calvinism, resulting in strong opposition from Old Light ministers like Jedidiah Morse (1761–1826), himself a renowned geographer. In 1819, the minister William Ellery Channing (1780–1842) elaborated to a Baltimore congregation upon the key tenets of Unitarianism, including the unity of God, the humanity of Jesus, individual free will, and the ethical qualities of Christianity.

By the 1830s, many Congregationalist churches in Massachusetts had assumed a Unitarian identity. There were some Unitarians, however, who saw this institutional growth as detrimental to the liberal origins of the movement. In 1838, during an address to the Harvard Divinity School, the poet and essayist Ralph Waldo Emerson (1803–82) criticized Unitarians for retaining too many features of "historical Christianity" and not focusing enough on "the soul of man." Emerson's development of a Transcendentalist philosophy stemmed from other romantic philosophical traditions in Germany and England, which questioned the certitude of Enlightenment empiricism and championed the subjectivity of personal experience.

Emerson's ideas inspired a small but influential generation of American thinkers and activists in the nineteenth century. The Transcendentalist Henry David Thoreau (1817–62) reacted to Emerson's essays *Nature* (1836) and *Self-Reliance* (1841) with his own experiment in simple living. After residing in a cabin near Concord, Massachusetts, on-and-off for two years, Thoreau wrote the book *Walden; or, Life in the Woods* (1854), "because I wished to live deliberately, to front only the essential facts of life, and see if I could not learn what it had to teach, and not, when I came to die, discover that I had not lived." Thoreau also applied his Transcendentalist beliefs to the political realm with his essay *Resistance to Civil Government* (1849) and his ideas about civil disobedience. Another Transcendentalist-turned-activist was Margaret Fuller (1810–50), a journalist, abolitionist, and women's rights advocate from Cambridge, Massachusetts. Fuller was the first editor of the Transcendentalist journal *The Dial* and author of the book *Woman in the Nineteenth Century* (1845). Sometimes described as America's first feminist, she likened the equality of men and women to the equality of blacks and whites. In a phrase akin to other evangelical Protestant abolitionists, she wrote, "If the negro be a soul, if the woman be a soul, appareled in the flesh, to one Master only are they accountable."

Offshoots from Unitarianism included Universalism and Spiritualism. Early Universalist ministers like John Murray (1741–1815) and Hosea Ballou (1771–1852) balanced reason with revelation in their message of universal salvation and their rejection of eternal damnation. But unlike Unitarianism, which was dominated by elite Congregationalists in urban New England, Universalism attracted followers from middle- and lower-class Protestant groups of Methodists and Baptists. By the 1840s, many of those who were sympathetic to Universalism gravitated to the ideas of Andrew Jackson Davis (1826–1910), a self-described "seer" from Poughkeepsie, New York, who popularized the belief in communication with the dead, also known as Spiritualism. Davis' advocacy for Spiritualism coincided with news of two sisters from Hydesville, New York – Kate (1837–92) and Margaret (1833–93) Fox – who claimed to communicate with spirits. Although it wasn't a formal denomination until the 1890s, Spiritualism proved appealing to many Americans who believed in the good of humanity and denied the finality of death. Spiritualists also became some of the most influential activists in the anti-slavery and women's rights movements. Many of the women who participated in the Seneca Falls Convention of 1848 – the first women's rights convention in the United States – and abolitionists like William Lloyd Garrison and the Grimké sisters embraced Spiritualism's radical respect for individual sovereignty.

It was in this atmosphere of religious experimentation that another new religious movement developed in the Burned-Over District of upstate New York. It came to be known as the Church of Jesus Christ of Latter-day Saints, but it is more commonly referred to as Mormonism. With its roots in the social upheaval of the Second Great Awakening and its sheer originality, many historians have described Mormonism as the quintessential American religion. It started with Joseph Smith (1805–44), the son of a failed farmer with a background in rural folk religion and evangelical Protestantism. In 1820, at the age of fourteen, Smith claimed to have received a vision of "the Father and the Son" and a message warning against denominational divisions. Over the next ten years, Smith experienced an epiphany of the angel Moroni, the supposed survivor of an ancient American tribe who provided a new revelation to Smith in the form of golden tablets inscribed in "Reformed Egyptian." Once translated, Smith called this new scripture *The Book of Mormon*, first published in 1830. Early followers regarded Smith as a prophet and believed that they were living in the End Times, thus the phrase "latter-day saints." Their millennial fervor was combined with a restorationist plea to return to the primitive Christianity of the New Testament.

Smith and other Mormon converts moved to Kirtland, Ohio, in 1830. Based on the continuing revelations of Smith, there they built the first Mormon temple, organized a system of communal property ownership, started to practice polygamy, and instituted new rituals known as "ordinances." At the same time, Mormon missionaries traveled to Great Britain and northern Europe. Still other Mormons settled in Missouri, believed to be the Garden of Eden. In 1839, as anti-Mormon sentiment grew in Ohio, Smith founded the city of Nauvoo on the banks of the Mississippi River in Illinois. Mormons envisioned the city as the New Jerusalem, the place where Smith believed they would "be prepared in all things, against the day when tribulation and desolation are sent forth upon the wicked." Internal and external opposition to the Mormon experiment at Nauvoo grew throughout the early 1840s, leading Smith to order the destruction of the presses of a hostile newspaper and to announce his candidacy for president of the United States. The governor of Illinois charged Smith and his older brother Hyrum (1800–44) with treason and had them arrested. While incarcerated, a mob attacked the jail and shot the Smith brothers to death. Brigham Young (1801–77) succeeded Smith as Mormonism's new "Prophet, Seer, and Revelator," after which he led an "exodus" of Nauvoo's Mormons to the Great Salt Lake in 1846. The U.S. government recognized the Territory of Utah in 1850 and appointed Young as its governor. Under the autocratic leadership of Young, Utah operated as a Mormon theocracy, ultimately resulting in armed confrontations between Mormon pioneers and U.S. military forces during the 1850s.

Mormonism wasn't the only alternative millennialist movement to develop during the Second Great Awakening. Following the events of the Cane Ridge Revival of 1801, Barton W. Stone (1772–1844) eschewed his affiliation with Presbyterianism and organized followers into a group simply called "Christians." Thomas Campbell and his son Alexander Campbell (1788–1866) established a similar group called the "Christian Association." By 1831, associates of Campbell and Stone merged their efforts to reject formal denominational organizations in favor of a restored version of primitive Christianity that emphasized the rituals of immersion baptism and the Lord's Supper. The Stone-Campbell movement, as it came to be known, promoted the postmillennialist view that human activities anticipated the Second Coming of Jesus.

The Baptist preacher William Miller (1782–1849) took millennial prophecies to new levels with his prediction that the Second Coming would take place in March of 1843. With the aid of a prominent publicist, Miller reached national audiences with his premillennialist prediction that the Second Coming of Jesus would begin the End Times. When the supposed date of the Second Coming came and went, Miller recalculated the date to March 22, 1844. Again, nothing happened, and the event came to be known as the "Great Disappointment." Those who remained steadfast in their support for Miller's premillennialism coalesced around the prophet and visionary Ellen Gould Harmon White (1827–1915), who would found the Seventh-Day Adventist Church in 1860.

Several utopian societies also gained membership in the nineteenth century. Millennialism and perfectionism, both hallmarks of the Second Great Awakening, proved crucial to the attractiveness of two groups in particular, the Shakers and the Oneida community. Following the death of the English immigrant and revelator Ann Lee (1736–84), a small cohort organized the United Society of Believers in Christ's Second Appearing in 1787. With connections to the Shaking Quakers – given the name because of their practice of trembling and convulsing during worship – they came to be known as Shakers. Shakers believed in Lee's revelation that sex was the primary source of human depravity. As such, they were called to live celibate lives in anticipation of the Second Coming. By 1825, as many as twenty Shaker communities thrived in the revival districts of New England, New York, Ohio, Kentucky, and Indiana. Another communitarian group, which came to be known as the Oneida community, also took an unorthodox attitude toward sexual relationships. John Humphrey Noyes (1811–86), a convert of Finney's, believed that those who experienced a conversion were forever free from sin. But in order to avoid the contamination of the unregenerate world, Noyes insisted that his followers combine their property and live together in Oneida, New York. There he instituted the controversial practice of "complex marriage," which amounted to each man being the husband of every woman and each woman being the wife of every man. This form of "sexual communion," according to Noyes, constituted a perfect form of partnership and mutuality that reinforced the belief that the Second Coming of Jesus had already occurred in A.D. 70. Under pressure from outside critics, Noyes abandoned the practice of complex marriage in 1879, followed by the dissolution of community property ownership.

IMMIGRATION, EXPANSION, AND RELIGIOUS DIVERSITY

During the antebellum period, the population of the United States grew from approximately 5.3 million in 1800 to over 31 million in 1860. It was also during this period that the territory of the United States expanded to the Pacific Ocean with the Louisiana Purchase of 1803 and the treaty ending the Mexican–American War in 1848. The combination of foreign immigration and the annexation of western lands generated a rise in religious diversity throughout much of the United States. Roman Catholics and Jews immigrated from Europe at unprecedented levels, as did people from China and other Asian countries (we'll cover Asian immigration in the next chapter). Native Americans and Mexicans also faced challenges as Protestant Americans migrated to territories west of the Mississippi River. In all of these cases, we have to consider the extent to which these newcomers assimilated to an American society so deeply influenced by a Protestant moral establishment.

Small numbers of Jews arrived in the British colonies during the seventeenth and eighteenth centuries. With few rabbis, Jews took it upon themselves to establish congregations in New York City (1656); Newport, Rhode Island (1677); Savannah, Georgia (1733); Philadelphia, Pennsylvania, (1745); and Charleston, South Carolina (1750). By 1800, approximately 1,600 Jews lived in the United States. Most of them were Ashkenazic Jews from northern Europe, although there were also Sephardic Jews from Spain. This number grew to around 150,000 by 1860, spurred in large part by the influx of German-speaking Jews. The ethnic diversity of American Judaism increased even more with the arrival of Yiddish-speaking Jews from Eastern Europe during the late-nineteenth and early-twentieth centuries.

Jewish communities responded to life in the United States with a combination of resistance and assimilation. Rebecca Gratz (1781–1869), a Jewish educator and philanthropist from Philadelphia, was influenced by the wave of Christian benevolent societies during the Second Great Awakening. She worked with Jewish and Christian women of Philadelphia to found the nonsectarian Female Association for the Relief of Women and Children in Reduced Circumstances in 1801. She also founded charitable societies in Philadelphia that were focused solely on the growing Jewish population, including the Female Hebrew Benevolent Society (1819), the Hebrew Sunday School (1838), and the Jewish Foster Home (1855). Isaac Leeser (1806–68), a cantor at Philadelphia's Congregation Mikveh Israel, supported Gratz's educational initiatives by publishing the *Hebrew Spelling-Book* in 1838, the first Hebrew primer for Jewish children in the United States. Leeser published and translated many other works with Jewish audiences in mind, including the first English translation of the Hebrew Bible (known as the "Leeser Bible") and the first American Jewish newspaper (*The Occident*). Always a defender of Jewish interests in a predominantly Gentile (non-Jewish) country, Leeser once petitioned Congress when a group of Presbyterians offered an amendment to the Constitution that called for the establishment of "a Christian government" in the United States. Writing on behalf of forty

Jewish congregations, Leeser argued for "the full right of every man to worship God as his conscience impels him."

Another innovative navigator of the Protestant-dominated public sphere was Isaac Mayer Wise (1819–1900), the leading advocate of Reform Judaism in nineteenth-century America. Born in Bohemia, Wise immigrated to New York in 1846 and ultimately accepted a rabbi position at Cincinnati's Congregation Bene Yeshurun in 1853. There he sought to reform Judaism in order to meet what he saw as the challenges of the modern world. Specifically, he encouraged Jews to pray in their vernacular language (usually English or German, instead of Hebrew); divest themselves of distinctive cultural practices associated with Jewish clothing and dietary restrictions; and allow men and women to sit together in pews. His national influence grew as he started publishing the newspaper *The Israelite* in 1854; released the *Minhag America* in 1857, which was a Jewish prayer book tailor-made for American Jews; participated in theological debates between Jews and Christians with books like *The Essence of Judaism* (1861) and *The Origin of Christianity* (1868); and founded Hebrew Union College (1875), which was America's first Jewish seminary. Yet many of his ideas produced controversy within American Jewish circles. For instance, he believed that the United States was the new Zion and Washington, D.C., the new Jerusalem. This meant that he opposed the establishment of an independent Jewish state, which drew the ire of many Jews who still saw Palestine as the Chosen Land of the Israelites. And in 1883, Wise refused to apologize to a group of observant Jews after serving them *trayf* – food such as shrimp and crab that broke Jewish law – at a banquet for the first graduating class of Hebrew Union College. Wise dismissed the incident as "kitchen Judaism," but it portended greater divisions among American Jews later in the nineteenth century.

As we've already seen in Chapter Three, Catholics from Spain and France colonized parts of North America long before there was even a concept of the United States. In the British colonies, most Catholics lived in Maryland. Founded by the Anglo-Catholic Calvert family in 1634, Maryland attracted other Anglo-Catholic immigrants because of its openness to religious tolerance as instituted by the colony's "Act Concerning Religion" in 1649. While Protestants ultimately curtailed many of the legal provisions for

Catholic inhabitants by the end of the seventeenth century, Maryland remained unique in British North America for its sizeable Catholic population. It was no accident, then, that Maryland produced the only Catholic to sign the Declaration of Independence, Charles Carroll (1737–1832), and the first Catholic bishop of the United States, John Carroll (1735–1815). Anglo-Catholic citizens of the nascent United States were typically supportive of the American principles of freedom and democracy, which historians have described as "republican Catholicism." But they also bought and sold slaves like many white Protestants. Jesuit priests, in particular, constituted one of the largest slaveholding entities in antebellum Maryland.

Following the events of the French Revolution, twenty-three French priests immigrated to the United States during the 1790s at the invitation of John Carroll, the bishop of the Diocese of Baltimore. This move doubled the number of priests in the United States. It also led to the recruitment of over one hundred more French priests and the education of many more American-born priests in seminaries. These French and French-trained priests were responsible for spreading a Tridentine form of Catholicism that looked to the pope in Rome for authority. Tension between republican Catholicism and Tridentine Catholicism arose over the common American practice of trusteeism, which gave legal control over church property and administration to laypeople. John England (1786–1842), the first bishop of the Diocese of Charleston, took a republican approach to church leadership when he issued a constitution in 1823 that called on the laity and the clergy to share authority over church matters. This approach contrasted with the French way of centralizing authority in the clergy and questioning the democratic ethos of their Anglo-American counterparts.

Between 1776 and 1820, the Catholic population in the United States grew from approximately 25,000 to 150,000. Areas of concentration included the southern states of Maryland, Kentucky, and Louisiana, as well as urban centers in the North. By 1850, the Catholic Church was the single largest religious institution in the United States, surpassing all other Protestant denominations in overall membership. What caused this incredible growth? Immigration. Irish Catholics constituted the largest ethnic group to immigrate to the United States, with approximately 4.3 million making the journey between 1820 and 1920. Other ethnic Catholic groups included Germans (1.6 million); Italians (4.1 million); Poles (2.1 million); French Canadians (1 million); Mexicans (500,000); and other Eastern Europeans (Slovaks, Czechs, Lithuanians, and Ruthenians). All told, almost 16 million Catholics resided in the United States by 1920, accounting for seventeen percent of the total population.

Given these statistics, the Catholic Church in nineteenth-century America was an immigrant church. These immigrants typically lived in cities like New York and New Orleans, where they organized into national parishes according to ethnicity. The "ethnic village" became a hallmark of urban living for many Catholics, which, according to the historian Jay Dolan, effectively "reinforced the ethnic differences of the people and enabled neighborhoods to build cultural barriers among themselves." Cultural differences were reinforced by language barriers, with twenty-eight languages spoken in Catholic churches throughout the United States by the end of the nineteenth century. Church parishes provided ethnic Catholics, many of whom were from lower-class laboring families, with social, medical, and educational services that were otherwise unavailable. Women religious orders like the Sisters of Charity and the Carmelites were especially important to the success of these and other Catholic initiatives to supply both secular and religious support to the laity. The church parish served as the primary site of liturgical and sacramental life for Catholics, including the most common rituals of baptism, confession, communion, confirmation, and marriage. That being said, Catholics also extended their religious beliefs and practices to their homes and neighborhoods. Devotion to the Virgin Mary and other saints, for example, was a popular form of Catholic expression that didn't always require the oversight of priests and that allowed for a diverse range of ethnic-specific practices.

The expanding size of the Catholic Church in the United States, combined with its growing political power, sparked nativist fears among many Protestant Americans. In his book *Foreign Conspiracy against the Liberties of the United States* (1835), the inventor and anti-Catholic activist Samuel F. B. Morse (1791–1872) differentiated between "Popery, from its very nature, favoring despotism, and Protestantism, from its very nature, favoring liberty." The nativist newspaper *American Protestant Vindicator* popularized anti-Catholicism for national audiences, as did exposés of supposedly licentious priests and nuns in books like *The Awful Disclosures of Maria Monk* (1836). Literary antagonism toward the Catholic Church sometimes fueled outright violence against Catholics. In 1834, a Protestant mob burned down an Ursuline convent in Charlestown, Massachusetts, just one day after Lyman Beecher delivered a sermon to several Congregationalist churches in Boston, in which he warned that "despotic princes in Europe … could they by means of the Romish church, subvert our free institutions and bring into disgrace all ideas of effective government." Other anti-Catholic riots took place in cities like Philadelphia and New York, while members of the Know-Nothing Party won state and national offices by running on an anti-Catholic political platform.

Also of concern to many Protestants was the spread of Catholicism to the western half of the continent. Again, Lyman Beecher, in his book *A Plea for the West* (1835), articulated one of the more popular renderings of anti-Catholic paranoia with his conspiratorial character-ization of immigrant hordes flooding the American frontier. Addi-tionally, with the 1848 Treaty of Guadalupe Hidalgo and the 1854 Gadsden Purchase, the United States acquired former Mexican territories with a long history of Catholicism. The Catholic Church quickly established new dioceses in Galveston (1847), Santa Fe (1853), and San Francisco (1853), and subsequently assigned European and American priests and nuns to attend to the indigenous and emigrant Catholic populations. There many Catholic newcomers joined Protestants in criticizing Mexican Catholics for their extra-liturgical devotional practices and inattention to the dictates of the American archbishop of Baltimore and the Italian pope in Rome. Devotion to Our Lady of Guadalupe, the Catholic patroness of Mexico, was especially important to Hispanic residents of the expanding United States, with many churches and shrines dedicated to this particular manifestation of the Virgin Mary throughout the region.

Domestic missionaries followed the greater migration of Americans into the trans-Mississippi West, many of whom concentrated their evangelization efforts on Native American groups. The Boston-based American Board of Commissioners of Foreign Missions (ABCFM) committed a considerable amount of resources to the evangelization of Indian tribes like the Cherokee, Dakota, and Ojibwe, as did other domestic missionary societies. From his postmillennialist perspective, the ABCFM official Jeremiah Evarts (1781–1831) believed that it was necessary to convert the "pagan" Indians of the United States in order to prepare for the return of Jesus Christ. Evarts, as well as many other evangelical Protestant missionaries, also opposed the Indian Removal Act of 1830, which authorized the federal government to relocate Native American groups to territories west of the Mississippi River. "May a gracious Providence avert this country from the awful calamity of exposing ourselves to the wrath of heaven," Evarts wrote, "as a consequence of disregarding the cries of the poor and defenceless [sic] [Indians]." Evarts' position on Indian removal was a minority one, however. Still more Americans agreed with what the journalist John O'Sullivan (1813–95) described as America's "manifest destiny to spread and to possess the whole of the continent which Providence has given us for the development of the great experiment of liberty."

Whether forcibly relocated or indigenous to the West, many Native Americans adapted aspects of their traditional religious beliefs and practices to the Christian messages of domestic missionaries. This process of "religious syncretism," according to the historian Christine Heyrman, generated "a creative combination of the elements of different religious traditions yielding an entirely new religious system capable of commanding broad popular loyalties." An example of this kind of syncretism occurred in the Cherokee tribe during the 1850s. The Baptist missionary Evan Jones (1788–1872) managed to convert some Cherokees to Christianity after he traveled eight hundred miles from Georgia to Oklahoma along the notorious "Trail of Tears." An abolitionist, Jones barred Cherokee slaveholders from joining his mission churches. He also encouraged Cherokee men to join the secretive Keetoowah Society, which merged traditional native and Christian beliefs into a movement focused on the preservation of the Cherokee people during the politically tumultuous years leading up the American Civil War.

Catholic priests and nuns joined their Protestant rivals in developing Indian missions in the West. Sister Rose Philippine Duchesne (1769–1852), member of the Religious Sisters of the Sacred Heart of Jesus, was one such Catholic missionary who worked among the recently relocated Potawatomi tribe in Kansas during the 1840s. Like her male missionary counterparts, Duchesne deplored the federal government's forced removal of the Potawatomi from their homes in Indiana. She and her fellow nuns established a school for Potawatomi girls and provided medical treatment to those in need. Approximately one hundred Potawatomi attended mass and received the sacraments on a regular basis, out of a total population of approximately eight hundred. Potawatomi converts to Catholicism also lived in a separate village from those who remained unbaptized, although they continued to interact with each other during traditional Potawatomi ceremonies.

Western migration, like European immigration, highlights the incredible level of religious entanglement and innovation in nineteenth-century America. By the time the Civil War ended in 1865, while white Protestants continued to dominate much of the social and cultural fabric of American life, the religious composition of the United States had never been more diverse. And while we've already covered several topics that took place after the 1860s, the next chapter will provide a thorough analysis of how the rise of religious diversity continued to challenge conceptions of what it meant to be American in an increasingly urban, industrial, and modern nation.

SUMMARY

- The American War of Independence was a political revolution and military confrontation that involved Christians on all sides of the conflict. The diverse claims of Protestants and Deists contributed to the ratification of the First Amendment to the Constitution, which set the foundation for legal arguments over the establishment and free exercise of religion in the United States.

- Protestant denominations experienced unprecedented growth in the early American republic, especially those associated with evangelical forms of Protestantism. Methodists, Baptists, and Presbyterians, in particular, gained considerable religious popularity and political influence during a period that would come to be known as the Second Great Awakening.

- African Americans were not immune to the religious revivalism of the Second Great Awakening. Free and enslaved blacks applied their understanding of Christianity both to the abolitionist movement and everyday life on plantations. White Americans were generally split over the question of slavery along sectional lines between North and South, though many identified with the principles of evangelical Protestantism.

- The first half of the nineteenth century was marked by incredible religious experimentation among groups that deviated from orthodox forms of Christianity. These new religious movements included Transcendentalism, Universalism, Spiritualism, and Mormonism, as well as other communitarian groups that sought to create utopian societies.

- European immigration contributed to the ethnic and religious diversification of the American religious landscape during the nineteenth century. Roman Catholic and Jewish immigrants reacted to life in the United States with a combination of assimilation and resistance, while many Protestant Americans responded to these changes in religious demographics with xenophobia and nativism.

- Many Americans viewed the territorial expansion of the United States as a means to spread Christianity throughout the continent of North America. It was in the American West that Protestant and Catholic missionaries worked with and sometimes against the state to evangelize Native Americans and Mexicans, peoples who had inhabited these lands for centuries.

FURTHER READING

For studies of religion and the founding of the United States, see Frank Lambert, *The Founding Fathers and the Place of Religion in America* (Princeton, NJ: Princeton University Press, 2006); Thomas Kidd, *God of Liberty: A Religious History of the American Revolution* (New York: Basic Books, 2012); and Henry May, *The Enlightenment in America* (New York: Oxford University Press, 1976). For works on religion in the new American republic, see Amanda Porterfield, *Conceived in Doubt: Religion and Politics in the New American Nation* (Chicago: University of Chicago Press, 2012); Nathan Hatch, *The Democratization of American Christianity* (New Haven, CT: Yale University Press, 1991); Paul Johnson, *A Shopkeeper's Millennium:*

Society and Revivals in Rochester, New York, 1815–1837 (New York: Hill and Wang, 1978); and Christine Leigh Heyrman, *Southern Cross: The Beginnings of the Bible Belt* (Chapel Hill: University of North Carolina Press, 1997).

For insight into the relationship between religion and race, see Albert Raboteau, *Slave Religion: The "Invisible Institution" in the Antebellum South* (New York: Oxford University Press, 1978); Yvonne Chireau, *Black Magic: Religion and the African American Conjuring Tradition* (Berkeley: University of California Press, 2006); and Randall Miller, Harry Stout, and Charles Reagan Wilson, eds., *Religion and the American Civil War* (New York: Oxford University Press, 1998). For books about the new religious movements of the nineteenth century, see Catherine Albanese, *The Spirituality of the American Transcendentalists* (Macon, GA: Mercer University Press, 1988); Ann Lee Bressler, *The Universalist Movement in America, 1770–1880* (New York: Oxford University Press, 2000); Ann Braude, *Radical Spirits: Spiritualism and Women's Rights in Nineteenth-Century America* (Bloomington: Indiana University Press, 2001); and Jan Shipps, *Mormonism: The Story of a New Religious Tradition* (Urbana: University of Illinois Press, 1987). For information about Jews and Catholics in nineteenth-century America, see Jonathan Sarna, *American Judaism: A History* (New Haven, CT: Yale University Press, 2005); Leonard Dinnerstein, *Anti-Semitism in America* (New York: Oxford University Press, 1995); John McGreevy, *Catholicism and American Freedom: A History* (W.W. Norton, 2004); and Jay Dolan, *In Search of an American Catholicism: A History of Religion and Culture in Tension* (New York: Oxford University Press, 2002).

5

RELIGION IN A MODERNIZING AMERICA, 1860s TO 1920s

The events of the American Civil War were both destructive and transformative for those who lived in the United States. No group was more involved in picking up the pieces of war than recently freed African Americans, many of whom looked to religious organizations for spiritual and practical support in a country still steered by racism and white supremacy. Scientific and technological advances – the fruits of which included the theory of evolution and the industrialization of the economy – compelled many Americans to reconsider the role of religion in a modernizing nation. Some Christians recoiled from the changes that came with the times and found refuge in conservative forms of evangelical Protestantism and charismatic movements like Pentecostalism. Others applied liberal interpretations of Christianity to meet the challenges of poverty and inequality in both urban and rural America. All the while, the tide of European immigration continued to increase the ethnic and religious diversity of the United States, with Catholics and Jews adapting their respective religious beliefs and practices to suit their material circumstances. It was also during this period that the U.S. government issued laws that restricted the immigration of non-Europeans, but not before Hinduism, Buddhism, and other Asian religious traditions grabbed the attention of religiously curious white Americans. And with a population of fewer than 400,000 by the turn of the century, many Native Americans organized pan-Indian revitalization movements as a way to restore cosmic and political order to indigenous communities.

RELIGION AND RACE AFTER THE CIVIL WAR

Upon learning of the fall of Richmond, Virginia, in April of 1865, President Abraham Lincoln insisted that he visit the former capital of the Confederate States of America. News of his impending arrival spread quickly among the African American residents of the city. In a dispatch to the *Philadelphia Press*, the black journalist Thomas Morris Chester (1834–92) reported that Lincoln's arrival in Richmond had "never before presented such a spectacle of jubilee." The euphoric crowd, according to Chester, was overwhelmingly composed of "American citizens of African descent," many of whom likened Lincoln to a messiah and shouted praise to God for their freedom. In the days that followed, "the colored churches ... were densely populated with delighted audiences," described by Chester as a "redeemed people" eager to celebrate the end of the war in their own houses of worship. Many white residents, not surprisingly, weren't pleased about the turn of events. According to Chester, one "female aristocrat" screamed from her window, "I will die and go to hell before I would take the oath" of allegiance to the United States, while another woman, upon hearing of General Robert E. Lee's (1807–70) surrender, announced that she "would rather see him in hell than marched through the streets of Richmond."

The events of Richmond's surrender speak to the religious and racial divisions that would impact the lives of every American after the Civil War. The emancipation of almost four million slaves of African descent set in motion incredible changes to the social and economic futures of both the South and the North. White reactions to these changes were mixed, with some working to restrict the civil rights of blacks and others encouraging racial integration. Advances in racial equality during the period of Reconstruction (1865–77) quickly deteriorated during the era of Jim Crow (1877–1965), a time that saw racial segregation legalized and violence against blacks rise throughout the United States. Religion figured prominently in both black and white efforts to make sense of this changing world.

As discussed in the previous chapter, whites and blacks often worshiped in racially integrated churches throughout the antebellum South. After the Civil War, however, racial segregation of churches became the norm. Independent black religious organizations provided African Americans with communities of support that came in the form of both spiritual welfare and social services. These same religious organizations produced many black politicians who were elected to office at the local, state, and national levels during Reconstruction. For example, the first African American in the U.S. Senate was the African Methodist Episcopal minister Hiram Revels (1827–1901) of Mississippi. With the rise of white supremacist organizations like the Ku Klux Klan, black churches also tried to protect their congregations from racist acts of violence and terrorism.

White denominations in the North sent over seven thousand domestic missionaries to serve the needs of freed men and women in the South. The Congregationalist-sponsored American Missionary Association was one such organization that established schools and other social services for blacks in both rural and urban areas of the South. Protestant women, in particular, served as teachers to the largely illiterate and under-educated African American population. Martha Hale Clary, for instance, left the Massachusetts-based Mount Holyoke Female Seminary when she was twenty-four years old and moved to Beaufort, South Carolina, where she established a school for the Gullah and other freed people of the area. By the 1870s, African American women were assuming the role of teacher to both the children and adults of South Carolina. Caroline Putnam, formerly an Oberlin College student and anti-slavery activist, moved to Virginia after the Civil War and built a school for African Americans. After the fall of Reconstruction and the rise of Jim Crow, Putnam became even more strident in her defense of the legal and political rights of African Americans, including her support for the creation of the National Association for the Advancement of Colored People (NAACP).

White Christian southerners responded to the defeat of the Confederacy both with nostalgia for the past and visions for the future. The big three Protestant denominations – Baptists, Methodists, and Presbyterians – remained divided along sectional lines and effectively merged evangelicalism with racism in the South. Even in defeat, white southerners preserved their commitment to Confederate nationalism and produced what the historian Charles Reagan Wilson described as "the religion of the Lost

Cause," or the belief that God was on the side of the Confederates even though they had lost the war. Known as the poet-priest of the South, the Irish-Catholic Father Abram Ryan (1838–86) was one among many acolytes of the Lost Cause who wrestled with the consequences of defeat. In one particular poem entitled *The Prayer of the South*, Ryan wrote: "Forgive my foes – they know not what they do – / Forgive them all the tears they made me shed;/ Forgive them, though my noblest sons they slew,/And bless them, though they curse my poor, dear dead." Ryan's "foes" were Union soldiers from the North. Yet as time went on – and especially after the repeal of Reconstruction and America's involvement in global conflicts like the Spanish–American War and World War I – reconciliation between white northerners and white southerners became possible. According to the historian Edward Blum, sectional reunion depended on "the conflation of whiteness, American nationalism, Protestant Christianity, and global imperialism," all of which reinforced the institution of Jim Crow laws in both the North and the South.

When the U.S. Supreme Court ruled in *Plessy v. Ferguson* (1896) that racial segregation was constitutionally protected, black churches became even more central to the religious and social lives of African Americans. Black church membership grew from 2.6 million in 1890 to 3.6 million in 1906. The National Baptist Convention, founded in 1895, was the largest black denomination in the United States at the turn of the century, followed by a variety of Methodist and independent denominations. These and other churches served as centers of activism against the lynching of African Americans by white vigilantes. Ida B. Wells (1862–1931), a journalist and early civil rights leader, was one of the most famous critics of lynching, who believed that she was called to "show that the Afro-American race is more sinned against than sinning." The Georgia Baptist minister William Jefferson White also reacted to lynching and other forms of racial injustices both from the pulpit and the press. He published the black newspaper *Georgia Baptist*, worked with W. E. B. Du Bois to found the Georgia Equal Rights League, and co-founded the Augusta Theological Institute (later renamed Morehouse College). In these and other cases, African American Christians fused their religious and political beliefs into a form of civil rights activism that relied on the organizational power of black churches.

While African Americans pursued advances in civil rights, a new religious movement known as Pentecostalism also gained the attention of many blacks who were looking for religious renewal. Early Pentecostalism was a restorationist movement with roots in Methodism. As the name implies, Pentecostalism emphasizes events depicted in the New Testament, in which the Holy Spirit descended upon Jesus's apostles on Pentecost and Paul described the gifts of the Holy Spirit to followers of Jesus. For Pentecostals, the most important gifts of the Holy Spirit are speaking in tongues (also known as glossolalia), interpreting tongues, prophesying, and healing. Charles Harrison Mason (1864–1961), a Tennessee native and son of slaves, founded the Church of God in Christ in 1897, ultimately becoming the most influential black Pentecostal denomination in the United States. According to the historian Anthea Butler, female members, and especially those with the status of "church mother," "formed the backbone of the Church of God in Christ" and set the standard for "piety, devotion, and civic life" in black Pentecostal communities.

In 1906, William J. Seymour (1870–1922), an African American holiness preacher from Louisiana, introduced the beliefs and practices of Pentecostalism to a small black church on Azusa Street in Los Angeles. A revival started soon thereafter, receiving national attention for its multiculturalism (participants included whites, blacks, Latinos, and Asians), and ecstatic displays of glossolalia. Charles Fox Parham (1873–1929), a white Pentecostal minister who opened a Bible school in Topeka, Kansas, visited Azusa Street to see the revival for himself. His observations were both dismissive – he characterized Seymour's influence as "spiritual power prostituted" – and racist – he described the revival as "darkey camp meeting stunts." Parham's racist attitude highlighted a general split within Pentecostalism along black and white lines that persisted throughout the twentieth century.

That being said, the Canadian evangelist Aimee Semple McPherson (1890–1944) spread the Pentecostal message of Holy Spirit baptism to inter-racial audiences at camp revivals throughout the United States and with her establishment of the Angelus Temple in Los Angeles in 1923. McPherson's church attracted a weekly attendance of up to fifty thousand people during the 1920s. She also reached national audiences with her monthly magazine *Bridal Call* (she liked to describe herself as the "Bride of Christ") and radio station KFSG (Kall Four Square Gospel). While most people remember her for disappearing from a California beach and reappearing in Mexico under mysterious circumstances in 1926, McPherson nonetheless stood out for her unique ability to spread Pentecostalism with the help of new media, business acumen, and a charismatic personality.

From 1910 to 1930, approximately 1.5 million African Americans migrated from the South to the North and parts of the West. Historians refer to this movement of people as the Great Migration. And while three-quarters of African Americans still remained in the South, those who resettled in places like Chicago, New York, and Detroit contributed to the overall urbanization of the United States during the early twentieth century. Some African Americans likened their migration to that of the Israelites fleeing slavery in Egypt and reaching the Promised Land. Once out of the South, old and new black churches functioned as social service centers and spiritual oases for new migrants. Most black churches were affiliated with Baptist denominations, but there were also many so-called storefront churches scattered throughout urban streetscapes. Lucy Smith (1866–1952), a migrant from Georgia, opened a storefront church in Chicago called All Nations Pentecostal Church. She developed a reputation as a healer and encouraged ecstatic dance and song during worship services. Also like her contemporary McPherson, Smith took to the airwaves with her radio show, *The Glorious Church of the Air*, thereby extending her message of holiness throughout the Midwest and introducing audiences to the latest in gospel music.

A relatively small but influential number of African Americans participated in alternative religious movements that challenged common conceptions of race. In Harlem, New York, the Jamaican immigrant Marcus Garvey (1887–1940) established the Universal Negro Improvement Association, which ultimately grew to over seven hundred branches in thirty-eight states during the 1920s. The association's motto was "One God! One Aim! One Destiny!" which belied Garvey's intent for black Americans to resettle Africa in fulfillment of Psalm 68:31: "Princes shall come out of Egypt: Ethiopia shall soon stretch forth her hands unto God." At an association meeting in 1924, Garvey and his followers announced that Jesus was a "black man of sorrows" and Mary was a "black

Madonna," further reinforcing the fusion of Christianity and black nationalism among some African American circles. In Massachusetts, Charles Emmanuel Grace (1881–1960), also known as Sweet Daddy Grace, founded the United House of Prayer for All People in 1919. Although Grace promoted non-racial forms of fellowship, his ministry proved especially attractive to black Pentecostals. Grace's supposed ability to heal the sick and perform miracles led some followers to believe in the celebrity preacher's divinity.

Eschewing Christian connections to black identity were the Moorish Science Temple and the Nation of Islam. Timothy Drew (1886–1927), also known as Noble Drew Ali, claimed to be a prophet who taught that African Americans descended from North African Muslims. With little connection to traditional Islam, Drew's Moorish Science Temple recognized the religious authority of the prophet Muhammad, as well as Confucius, the Buddha, and Jesus. He published the *Circle Seven Koran* in 1927, which bore minimal connection to actual translations of the *Qur'an* and suggested that Jesus was a black prophet who set the stage for the rise of Islam. Following the death of Drew, the mysterious black prophet Wallace D. Fard established a temple in Detroit that identified Islam as the true religion of African Americans. Elijah Poole (1897–1975), also known as Elijah Muhammad, took leadership of Fard's nascent Nation of Islam during the 1930s and spread the messages of black nationalism, black self-independence, and white Christian injustice to African American communities.

WHITE PROTESTANT ALLIANCES AND DIVISIONS

The British naturalist Charles Darwin (1809–82) published *On the Origin of Species* in 1859. In it, he proposed an evolutionary theory of natural selection, effectively challenging the creationist belief in the divine origin of the universe. Christian responses to what would come to be known as Darwinism ranged from cautious support to rabid denunciation. The Harvard botanist Asa Gray (1810–88), while critical of Darwin's theory on several counts, spent much of his career reconciling evolutionary biology with Christian interpretations of creation. Specifically, Gray argued that God, as the designer of the universe, guided the evolution of creation. In the sixth edition of *Origin* (1872), even Darwin hinted that the "Creator" "breathed" life into nature and thus set in motion the process of natural selection. More conservative Christians viewed Darwin's theory as a contradiction to literal interpretations of the Genesis story of creation. In Darwin's world, humans weren't unique among other animals; they were just another species of beasts caught in a battle described by later sociologists as the "survival of the fittest."

Controversies over Darwinism were representative of a more general anxiety about the changing religious landscape of the United States at the turn of the century. Protestants reacted to these changes in ways which divided some believers into liberal and conservative camps. On the liberal end of the spectrum was the Social Gospel movement, which sought to save both individual souls and society at large in anticipation of the Kingdom of God on earth. On the conservative side were fundamentalism and Pentecostalism, with the former taking a firm doctrinal position against modernism and the latter emphasizing the personal experience of the Holy Spirit. Technological advances in mass media – radio, newspaper, film – contributed to the popularization of all three of these movements, resulting in both new alliances and divisions between Protestant sects in the United States.

Historians often cite the Connecticut pastor Horace Bushnell (1802–76) as the "father of American theological liberalism" for his criticism of Christian revivalism and promotion of Christian education. In his 1847 book *Christian Nurture*, Bushnell asked, "What is the true idea of Christian education?" Answer: "That the child is to grow up a Christian, and never know himself as being otherwise." He identified the home and the church as the primary sites of lifelong enculturation in the Christian faith. The "technical experience" of a sudden conversion, he argued, was not an ideal way for a sinner to join the Christian community. Instead, Bushnell advocated for an incremental unfolding of Christianity during childhood and then into adolescence and adulthood.

Bushnell's openness to gradual change anticipated liberal Protestant responses to biblical criticism and social Darwinism after the Civil War. Biblical criticism, also known as higher criticism, is the historical and literary analysis of scripture, which the scholar John Barton characterizes as "an open, rational approach, which treats the biblical texts like any other books from the ancient world."

This kind of attitude toward the Bible required a progressive and optimistic view of humanity, one that trusted Christians to do the work of God on earth. Yet while liberal Protestants were impressed by the work of biblical criticism, they were less enthusiastic about the libertarianism of those who applied Darwin's theory of natural selection to society and the economy. It was the British sociologist Herbert Spencer (1820–1903) who coined the phrase "survival of the fittest," which, among other things, meant that those who accrued wealth and power were more fit to survive in the competitive marketplace of modern society. The American sociologist William Graham Sumner (1840–1910), a former Episcopalian priest, extended Spencer's ideas of social Darwinism by supporting laissez-faire capitalism and disparaging the poor for their pleas for equality. "A drunkard in the gutter," Sumner bluntly argued, "is just where he ought to be."

Many liberal Protestants rejected social Darwinism and proposed what came to be known as the Social Gospel. Given the poverty that came with urbanization and industrialization, the Congregationalist minister Washington Gladden (1836–1918) argued for the rights of workers to organize unions in his book *Working People and Their Employers* (1876). He also advocated for the civil rights of women and African Americans, as well as cooperation between Protestants, Catholics, and Jews in facing the challenges of the day. Walter Rauschenbusch (1861–1918), a Baptist minister and theologian, rose to prominence as a leading activist in the Social Gospel movement when he served as pastor to German immigrants living in the slums of Hell's Kitchen, New York, during the 1880s. He wrote *Christianity and the Social Crisis* in 1907, in which he argued that the United States, and indeed the world, was going through a revolution comparable to the upheavals of the Renaissance and Reformation. Rauschenbusch insisted that Christians should respond to this crisis as Jesus did, as someone who lived not just to save souls, but to fix society. "The kingdom of God is still a collective conception," Rauschenbusch wrote, "involving the whole social life of man." It was not enough to save "human atoms," because there was an entire "social organism" that needed saving too. And if Rauschenbusch's postmillennialism wasn't already obvious, he concluded that "it is not a matter of getting individuals to heaven, but of transforming the life on earth into the harmony of heaven." The Social Gospel, in short, was a movement to prepare for the Kingdom of God in the here and now by eliminating the social sins of poverty and inequality.

The Social Gospel grew during a period described by historians as the Progressive Era (1880–1920) and in the context of a wider movement known as "Social Christianity." Progressivism was a social, political, and moral effort to address poverty, working conditions, race relations, immigration, women's rights, and other social concerns. Social Christianity referred to a variety of religious organizations (Young Men's Christian Association, Salvation Army, and other urban missions) motivated by the Christian message of mercy and action to revitalize society in the name of Jesus Christ. On the political left of Social Christianity was Jane Addams (1860–1935), the Nobel Peace Prize winner who was known for her social work in Chicago's Hull House, her feminist philosophy, and her pacifism during the Spanish–American War and World War I. Addams described her social work as "Christian humanitarianism." On the political right of Social Christianity was Josiah Strong (1847–1916), a Congregationalist minister whose goal was to "Americanize," "Christianize," and "Anglo-Saxonize" the unsettled territories of the West and the urban slums of the East. In his 1885 book *Our Country: Its Possible Future and Its Present Crisis*, Strong expressed his belief that "it is fully in the hands of the Christians of the United States, during the next fifteen or twenty years, to hasten or retard the coming of Christ's kingdom in the world." Standing in the way of the Second Coming, according to Strong, were Catholics, Mormons, socialists, and any other group that fell outside his understanding of Anglo-Saxon superiority.

Not all Protestants accepted the postmillennialist belief that humans could perfect society through Christian-inspired social reform. Dwight Moody (1837–99), the most famous urban revivalist of the late nineteenth century, epitomized the conservative Protestant attitude toward the modernization of the United States. "I look upon this world as a wrecked vessel," Moody is known to have proclaimed. "God has given me a lifeboat and said, 'Moody, save all you can.'" In other words, Moody held the premillennialist belief that the world was too messed up for humans to fix. It was time, therefore, to get back to the basics of saving souls before the Second Coming of Jesus. His message of salvation, combined with his emotional preaching style and entrepreneurial organization, appealed to rural migrants recently relocated in the urban North. It was in Chicago, the surging capital of the American Midwest, that Moody established the Moody Bible Institute as the headquarters of what would become a national and even international revival effort that reached millions of America's city-dwellers.

Protestant fundamentalism represented the conservative doctrinal response to the liberalism of the Social Gospel and Progressive movements. The inerrancy of the Bible was central to fundamentalist theology, as was the miraculous virgin birth of Jesus, the imminence of the Second Coming of Jesus, the atonement of Jesus's crucifixion, the validity of Jesus's miracle-making, and the resurrection of the body and soul of Jesus. From 1910 to 1915, conservative theologians published a twelve-volume set of ninety essays entitled *The Fundamentals*, which attacked higher criticism, socialism, evolutionism, Mormonism, Spiritualism, Roman Catholicism, atheism, and modernism, among other "isms." One of the most popular fundamentalist revivalists of the period was Billy Sunday (1862–1935), an ex-professional baseball player from Iowa who defined what was known at the time as "muscular Christianity." Sunday described himself as "God's grenadier," a soldier for Christ with a penchant for displays of physical prowess, emotional exhortations, and patriotic zeal. Protestant fundamentalists also embraced the dispensationalist teachings of the Englishman John Nelson Darby (1800–82). Based primarily on the Book of Daniel, dispensational premillennialism divided the entirety of history according to dispensations, or epochs, leading up to the Second Coming and the restoration of Paradise on earth. Believers in dispensationalism expected that faithful Christians would experience the Rapture (the raising of bodies into heaven), while everyone else suffered through times of tribulation after Jesus's return.

Divisions between liberal and fundamentalist Protestants reached a crescendo during the 1920s. Harry Emerson Fosdick (1878–1969), a Baptist-trained pastor of New York's First Presbyterian Church, summarized liberal attitudes toward the fundamentalist controversy in his 1922 sermon "Shall the Fundamentalists Win?" In it, Fosdick declared that "all Fundamentalists are conservatives, but not all conservatives are Fundamentalists." Fosdick believed that "the best conservatives can often give lessons to the liberals in true liberality of spirit, but the Fundamentalist program is essentially illiberal and intolerant." In addition to commenting on fundamentalism's ahistorical and literalist interpretation of scripture, Fosdick highlighted a brewing dispute over the teaching of modern biology in public schools and an impulse among fundamentalists to "set up in Protestantism a doctrinal tribunal more rigid than the pope's."

Fosdick's reference to science in the classroom anticipated the Scopes "Monkey" Trial of 1925. The case against John Scopes (1900–70), a high school biology teacher in Dayton, Tennessee, hinged on a state law that banned the teaching of evolution in public schools. Clarence Darrow (1857–1938), a longtime advocate of progressive causes, defended Scopes against a prosecution that included William Jennings Bryan (1860–1925), a former Democratic presidential candidate and Secretary of State who was one of the country's leading champions of Protestant fundamentalism. In the courtroom, both sides framed the case as a battle between religion and science. Outside the courtroom, fundamentalists prayed for the success of Bryan's crusade against evolution. Aimee Semple McPherson, for example, sent a telegram to Bryan during the trial, which read, "Ten thousand members of Angelus Temple with her millions of radio church membership send grateful appreciation of your lion hearted championship of the Bible against evolution and throw our hats in the ring with you." In the national media, many portrayals of fundamentalists were unfavorable at best and downright mocking at worst, with journalists like H. L. Mencken (1880–1956) of the *Baltimore Sun* ridiculing those who accepted Bryan's "theologic bilge" and "peculiar imbecilities."

Scopes was found guilty of teaching evolution, although the conviction was later overturned. Putting the legal decision aside, the court of public opinion reacted to the Scopes Trial with derision against Protestant fundamentalism. The historian George Marsden described the Scopes Trial as "a turning point for the [fundamentalist] movement" that compelled fundamentalists to retreat from the public sphere, but not without "relocating and building a substantial subculture" that would ultimately rise again in the 1950s. At the same time, liberal Protestants struggled to reconcile their progressive view of humanity in the aftermath of World War I and the Great Depression, leading many to reorient their theological perspectives to the shifting social, economic, and political landscape of the interwar years.

EUROPEAN IMMIGRATION AND ETHNIC DIVERSITY

As we covered in the previous chapter, European immigration contributed to the diversification of religion in the United States. Many Protestant Americans reacted to this diversity with suspicion and paranoia. Ethnic divisions within these immigrant groups generated a variety of strategies for assimilating to American society. During the nineteenth century, Catholic leaders and intellectuals debated the extent to which Catholic immigrants should assimilate to American society. Orestes Brownson (1803–76), a prominent American-born convert to Catholicism, argued for the "Americanization" of Catholic immigrants. However, many Irish Catholics, including Archbishop John Hughes (1797–1864) of New York, reacted with derision to Brownson's call for immigrants to "ultimately lose their own nationality and become assimilated in general character to the Anglo-American race." Another influential convert was Isaac Hecker (1818–88), who became a priest and founded the Missionary Society of Saint Paul the Apostle with the mission to reconcile the Catholic Church with the "national characteristics" of the United States.

By the end of the nineteenth century, some of the country's most influential Catholic leaders channeled the sentiments of Brownson and Hecker in response to the challenges of modernity. John Ireland (1838–1918), the Irish-born archbishop of St. Paul, Minnesota, encouraged Catholics to participate as full citizens in American public life. "Church and Age!" he once shouted to a gathering in Baltimore. "Unite them in the name of humanity, in the name of God…. Our place is in the world as well as in the sanctuary." James Gibbons (1834–1921), the American-born archbishop of Baltimore, registered a similar level of approval for Catholics to assert themselves in American politics and culture. Gibbons was especially supportive of Catholic involvement in labor unions and critical of the injustices of big business. His efforts even contributed to the 1891 publication of Pope Leo XIII's encyclical *Rerum Novarum*, which condemned socialism, identified the excesses of capitalism, advocated for the rights of workers to organize and own property, and set the stage for Catholics of the twentieth century to fight for social justice.

The progressive maneuvers of Catholic leaders like Ireland and Gibbons were met with opposition from other members of the clergy, the laity, and even the pope. At stake was the extent to which Catholicism could bend to American forms of government and social norms without defying Catholic teachings. In the 1895 encyclical *Longinqua Oceani*, Pope Leo XIII wrote that "It would be very erroneous to draw the conclusion that in America is to be sought the type of the most desirable status of the Church, or that it would be universally lawful or expedient for State and Church, to be, as in America, dissevered and divorced." In other words, the pope was arguing that the American model for separating church and state was not an ideal form of government, as long as the church in question was the Catholic Church. In 1899, the pope went a step further in the letter *Testem Benevolentiae*, in which he labeled "Americanism" a heresy and insisted that the true form of Catholicism was Roman, not American. The final blow to progressive Catholics like Ireland and Gibbons was Pope Pius X's encyclical *Pascendi Dominici Gregis* (1903), which condemned what he called the "errors of modernists" and rejected the teaching of modern philosophy in Catholic schools and communities. The Vatican denounced so-called modernists for their openness to seeing the Catholic Church as an historical and ever-changing religious institution, instead of a timeless vessel of Christian truth revealed by God and inscribed in dogma.

The Vatican's strong opposition to Americanism and modernism had a chilling effect on Catholic involvement in many of the social and economic challenges facing the United States during the early twentieth century. Moreover, as late as the 1920s – described as "the golden age of the Catholic parish" by the historian Jay Dolan – there remained "the persistence of the Catholic subculture with the ethnic and foreign complexion of the Catholic population." A revival of anti-Catholic nativism in the 1920s also contributed to the continuation of Catholics basing their lives in ethnic neighborhoods that were sometimes referred to as ghettos. While the Immigration Act of 1924 dramatically reduced the number of immigrants admitted to the United States, second- and third-generation immigrants continued to balance "Old World" models of Catholic organization and expression with "New World" pressures to acquiesce to life in a country on the precipice of the Great Depression.

Like Catholics, Jews held similar concerns about assimilation to American life. As covered in the previous chapter, Isaac Meyer

Wise was the leader of Reform Judaism in the United States, a Jewish tradition that was especially open to change in the face of the modern world. The immigration of approximately three million Jews to the United States between 1880 and 1920, however, represented a dramatic shift in the demographic makeup and direction of American Jewry. A majority of the newcomers were fleeing from anti-Semitic regimes in Russia and Eastern Europe. They were poor, with some of them illiterate and unskilled. Many turned to orthodox forms of Judaism and isolated themselves from much of American society in ethnic urban enclaves. Others abandoned Judaism entirely, in favor of social reform movements that were divested of religious affiliation. A third group emphasized the national characteristics of Judaism by advocating for the establishment of an independent Jewish state. By the 1920s, four out of five Jews in the United States were from Eastern European backgrounds. There were many more Orthodox Jews than Reform Jews, but even greater was the number of nonobservant Jews who largely avoided association with synagogues.

In the midst of such flux, a group of rabbis founded what came to be known as Conservative Judaism. It represented a "middle way" between Reform Judaism and Orthodox Judaism. For instance, Conservative Jews took *halacha* (Jewish law) seriously but not always literally, while also including both Hebrew and vernacular languages in worship services. At the core of Conservative Judaism was the synagogue-center, a venue that served the religious, recreational, and educational needs of Jews. Its creator, Mordecai Kaplan (1881–1983), wanted the facilities to cultivate Jewish identity in ways both cultural and religious. Kaplan would later start another Jewish movement known as Reconstructionism. While some Jews considered his ideas too radical – for instance, he rejected the idea of human relationships with a supernatural deity – Kaplan's Reconstructionism proved instrumental in merging American and Jewish identities through community organization. He was also a leading advocate for Jewish women's equality. After founding the Society for the Advancement of Judaism in New York City in 1922, he and his congregants were some of the first Jews to institute mixed sex seating. He was also the first rabbi to conduct a *Bat Mitvah* in the United States, which included his twelve-year-old daughter reciting the blessings and reading from the Torah just like her pubescent male counterparts did in *Bar Mitvahs*.

Like other ethnic newcomers, Orthodox Christians who immigrated to the United States experienced similar levels of cultural transition. Beginning in the late eighteenth century, Alaska was the first place where there was a sustained Eastern Orthodox presence in North America. Russian missionaries like Ivan Veniaminov (1797–1879) ministered to native Alaskans, ultimately establishing a diocese headquartered in New Archangel (Sitka), Alaska, during the 1840s. The diocesan center was relocated to San Francisco in 1874, and then to New York in 1905. The reason for this institutional move was the rise of Eastern European immigration to the east coast. By 1920, there were approximately 300 Eastern Orthodox parishes in the United States organized by nationality. Greek Orthodox Christians constituted the largest group with around 300,000 members, followed by Russians with 150,000 members and still smaller numbers among Serbian, Romanian, Albanian, Bulgarian, Belarusian, Ukrainian, and Syrian communities. Each of these national groups maintained varying degrees of connection with the Orthodox Christian churches of their homelands, all of which experienced considerable reorganization during the revolutionary years before and after World War I. When new immigration all but ended in the 1920s, first-generation Eastern Orthodox immigrants noticed a decline in regular adherence by their children and grandchildren, due in part to the establishment of suburban churches away from immigrant life in cities, the education of younger generations in American public schools, and increased marriages with Catholics and Protestants.

Some of the roots of Eastern Orthodoxy go back to 1054, when there was a split between Latin-speaking Christians of Western Europe and Greek-speaking Christians of Eastern Europe. Since then, the Patriarch of Constantinople has remained the most recognizable leader of Orthodox Christianity, although actual authority rests with the patriarchs and bishops of each respective national church. Orthodox Christianity is similar to Roman Catholicism in its practice of the sacraments, although variations do exist. For example, priests are permitted to marry before ordination and infants receive communion at the time of baptism. Two-dimensional paintings known as icons also distinguish Orthodox Christianity from Roman Catholicism, which can be found in the churches and homes of the devout. Many Orthodox Christian churches in the United States include Byzantine architectural styling, usually with rectangular or cruciform floor plans and with cupolas or onion-shaped domes. In an American context, many of these general characteristics of Orthodox Christianity were subject to variation and revision according to the national and ethnic peculiarities of the Eastern European diaspora.

ASIAN AND NATIVE AMERICAN RELIGIONS

Just as European immigration started to rise in the 1880s, Asian immigration took a precipitous decline following a series of exclusionary acts aimed at people of Chinese and Japanese descent. In 1890, the Chinese population in the United States reached just over 100,000, most of which was concentrated in California and other western states with ties to the gold rush of the mid-nineteenth century. By 1920, the Chinese population was down to around 60,000, due largely to the passage of the Chinese Exclusion Act of 1882. A similar trend applied to Japanese immigrants, most of whom were practitioners of Pure Land Buddhism. They first traveled to Hawaii in the 1860s and then to California by the end of the century. Reaching over 100,000 at one point, the number of Japanese immigrants fell after the Oriental Exclusion Act of 1924. The act, which was a smaller component of the much more comprehensive Johnson-Reed Immigration Act, deemed all Asian immigrants to be "undesirable" additions to American society.

Chinese immigrants imported a diverse range of religious traditions to the United States. Upwards of four hundred makeshift temples, along with a handful of more permanent structures like the T'ien Hou Temple of San Francisco (founded in 1852), dotted the Pacific coast wherever there were Chinese workers. These temples often blended aspects of Taoism, Confucianism, Pure Land Buddhism, and Chinese folk religion, depending on the backgrounds of Asian immigrants. A visit to a Chinese temple in the late nineteenth century could include Confucian ancestor veneration, Buddhist devotion to bodhisattvas, Taoist ceremonies of sacrifice to gods, and folk practices specific to any number of Chinese language and kinship groups. Merchant organizations in San Francisco's Chinatown supplied ethnic Chinese with the closest thing to formal sites of religious expression, usually on the upper floors of tenements and warehouses. Unlike in temples in China, however, there were few permanent priests to attend to the daily rhythm of communal prayer and ritual, usually leaving worship to the discretion of individual visitors.

Japanese immigrants maintained institutional ties to a form of Pure Land Buddhism known as Jodo Shinshu ("The True Pure Land School") and headquartered in Kyoto, Japan. As a branch of Mahayana ("Great Vehicle") Buddhism, Jodo Shinshu stresses devotion to Amida Buddha, the creator of a heaven-like pure land that is believed to be obtainable through the recitation of the *Nembutsu*, or the sacred phrase *Namo Amida Butsu* ("Homage to the Awakened One of Infinite Light and Love"). After 1898, with the arrival of two Jodo Shinshu missionaries in San Francisco, ethnic Japanese founded religious and social welfare institutions like the Young Men's Buddhist Association, the Buddhist Women's Association, the Buddhist Mission to North America (later renamed Buddhist Churches of America), and Jodo Shinshu temples. According to the historian Richard Seager, such organizations provided ethnic Japanese with a haven from anti-Asian agitation, while at the same time serving "as vehicles for Americanization" in the form of sports leagues, Boy Scout troops, and other modes of American entertainment, work, and leisure.

The influence of Asian religions in the United States was not restricted to the immigration of ethnic Chinese and Japanese. Indeed, American Buddhism can be traced to the early nineteenth century, when American Transcendentalists like Ralph Waldo Emerson, Henry David Thoreau, and Walt Whitman (1819–92) applied their limited knowledge of Buddhism and Hinduism to their poetic and intellectual contributions to an emerging American literary tradition. Later, in the 1870s, two people – a disaffected Presbyterian named Henry Steel Olcott (1832–1907) and a naturalized Russian immigrant named Helena Petrovna Blavatsky (1831–91) – founded the Theosophical Society in New York City. Followers of Theosophy subscribed to a hybrid form of Buddhism that also included features of Christianity, Judaism, and Hinduism, as well as elements of occultism, esotericism, and modern science. Blavatsky's eclectic ideas stemmed from her belief in Spiritualism and her extensive travel throughout Eastern Europe, the Middle East, and India. In 1880, Olcott and Blavatsky publicly professed their adherence to Buddhism while visiting a temple in Sri Lanka. Olcott's publication of the *Buddhist Catechism*, as well as sympathetic pieces about Buddhism in the society's official organ *The Theosophist*, contributed to the popularization of Buddhism for some American audiences.

Public attention to Buddhism, as well as other non-Western religions, reached a high point in 1893 with the World's Parliament of Religions. The Parliament took place in conjunction with the larger World's Columbian Exposition being held in Chicago. John Henry Barrows (1847–1902), a Presbyterian minister and chief organizer of the event, touted the Parliament as "a return to the primitive unity of the world." It opened with the chiming of a bell ten times in honor of the ten so-called world religions: Judaism, Christianity, Islam, Zoroastrianism, Confucianism, Taoism, Hinduism, Buddhism, Jainism and Shintoism. Although still dominated by English-speaking Christians, representatives from other religions delivered addresses to audiences of up to five thousand people. According to the historian Richard Seager, the Parliament marked "the beginning of the modern interreligious dialogue movement." Anagarika Dharmapala (1864–1933), a Theravada Buddhist intellectual and protégé of Olcott, and Soyen Shaku (1856–1919), a Rinzai Zen monk, used the venue as an opportunity to demystify their respective Buddhist traditions and make them relevant to modern Americans. After the Parliament, they conducted lectures on Buddhism throughout the United States. They were followed by Daisetz Teitero Suzuki (1870–1966), a Japanese Zen master who convinced the German-American writer Paul Carus (1852–1919) to publish and promote Buddhist texts for American readers.

Arguably the most celebrated non-Western speaker at the Parliament was Swami Vivekananda (1863–1902), a Hindu monk from India and founder of a monastic order called the Ramakrishna Mission. Vivekananda delivered a message of religious universalism that appealed to the Parliament's liberal-minded Christian audience, at one point receiving a two-minute standing ovation for merely saying "Sisters and brothers of America!" Vivekananda built on his popularity at the Parliament by founding the Vedanta Society in 1894, which attracted many Americans who were already influenced by new religious movements like Theosophy and Spiritualism. As was the case with Buddhism, several high-profile Hindu practitioners followed Vivekananda in introducing Americans to versions of Hinduism that usually stressed the inclusiveness of Hinduism and the inter-compatibility between the world's religions. However, not all of the publicity aimed at Hinduism and Indian culture was positive. The Asian Exclusion Act of 1917 effectively ended immigration from India, while anti-Hindu publications like Katherine Mayo's *Mother India* (1927) scandalized American readers with reports of idol worship, child prostitution, widow burning, and animal sacrifice.

Prior to Vivekananda's American debut, Hinduism garnered relatively little attention in the American public because of the low level of Indian immigration. That being said, there were some liberal Protestants of the early nineteenth century who exhibited interest in aspects of Hinduism. Some Unitarians, for example, appreciated the universalist ideas of the Bengali reformer Rommohan Roy (1772–1833), while some of the Transcendentalists read Hindu texts like the *Rig Veda*, the *Upanishads*, and the *Bhagavad Gita*. James Freeman Clarke (1810–88), a member of Emerson's Transcendental Club, included a chapter on "Brahmanism" in his book *Ten Great Religions* (1871), which identified the Brahman caste as the chief arbiter of Indian culture and the "Hindoo" religion as a philosophical system with roots in Aryan civilization and Vedic scriptures. Clarke based much of his analysis on the works of the German philologist Max Müller (1823–1900), who was one of the world's leading scholars of Sanskrit and comparative religion during the nineteenth century. Yet even Müller, writing about the World's Parliament of Religion, couldn't help but trade his scholarly objectivity for an excited claim that "beneath and behind all religions there is one eternal, one universal religion, a religion to which every man, whether black, or white, or yellow, or red, belongs or may belong." It was this kind of sympathetic appreciation of Indian culture that motivated many liberal Protestants and free thinkers in the United States to welcome the universalist message of Vivekananda and other Hindu intellectuals at the turn of the century.

Just as the United States was experiencing an uptick in overall foreign immigration, the number of Native Americans reached a nadir of around 375,000 by the end of the nineteenth century. The cumulative impact of years of Christian evangelization and government efforts to relocate and in some cases exterminate

Native American groups proved harmful to the survival of indigenous religious systems. Yet far from total destruction, Native Americans continued to challenge the American government's vision for Indian life with revitalization and resistance movements of their own. Such innovative measures dated back to at least the eighteenth century. During Pontiac's Rebellion of the 1760s, a Delaware prophet named Neolin received a message from the "Master of Life" that implored him to reject British rule or else suffer from the effects of disease and alcoholism. "As to those who come to trouble your lands," the Master of Life is supposed to have told Neolin, "drive them out, make war upon them. I do not love them at all; they know me not, and are my enemies." This call to revitalize indigenous Indian ways also applied to the Shawnee prophet named Tenskwatawa (1775–1836), who was the brother of the famed warrior Tecumseh (1768–1813). While in a trance, Tenskwatawa claimed to have been told by the Master of Life to form a pan-Indian alliance against foreign intruders to their lands. Together, Tecumseh and Tenskwatawa organized an Indian confederacy against American incursions into the West, partly on the basis of Tenskwatawa's status as a prophet.

Similar kinds of prophetic and revitalization movements continued throughout the nineteenth century. In Oregon Country, a Wanapum shaman named Smohalla (c. 1815–95) developed a following among the Nez Percé after claiming that he had died and was resurrected as God's prophet to native peoples. In defiance of his education at the hands of Catholic missionaries, Smohalla preached that Native Americans were the first people created by God, and that those of other races were created as punishment for defying indigenous ways of life. Just as Smohalla's influence reached a highpoint in the 1870s, a similar movement known as the "Ghost Dance" started to gain popularity in Nevada with the preaching of the Paiute visionary Wodziwob (d. 1872). His message was one of anticipation – deceased ancestors would one day return to this world – and restoration – together, the living and the dead would reclaim lands and property taken by the whites.

A second Paiute shaman named Wovoka (c. 1856–1932), also known as Jack Wilson, extended the Ghost Dance movement even further into the Great Plains during the 1890s. The performance of the Ghost Dance was similar to other round dance ceremonies.

According to Wovoka, those who performed the dance and refrained from warfare would one day be reunited with their ancestors and live forever free from the whites. The Lakota Sioux took the Ghost Dance in a militant direction when they introduced "ghost shirts" to the ritual, which were cloaks believed to be impenetrable to the bullets of white aggressors. The widespread popularity of the Ghost Dance compelled U.S. government officials to ban the practice, although it continued largely unabated. Tension reached a high point in South Dakota during the winter of 1890, when U.S. military forces massacred around 200 Lakota men, women, and children near Wounded Knee Creek. Many of them were wearing ghost shirts, which served to delegitimize the Ghost Dance movement among many native groups thereafter.

The parallel stories of Asian immigration and Native American displacement speak to the diversity and hostility of religion in America. While it is accurate to say that these minority groups introduced new religious beliefs and practices to American society, it is also necessary to observe how many Christian Americans reacted to them with fear and violence. Of course, this dynamic was nothing new, and it would continue throughout the twentieth century as the American religious landscape shifted under the weight of the Great Depression, World War II, the Civil Rights Movement, new immigration, and other social and political forces.

SUMMARY

- Many Christian Americans interpreted the events of the American Civil War as God's judgment on the United States. In the years following the war, white and black Americans typically worshiped in segregated churches, further exacerbating racial divisions among Christians in both the North and the South.
- African Americans established a variety of independent religious organizations during the late nineteenth and early twentieth centuries. Pentecostalism drew considerable attention from African Americans, as did black nationalist groups like the Nation of Islam.
- The United States experienced dramatic social and economic changes at the turn of the century. Historians typically distinguish between liberal and conservative reactions among white

Protestants to urbanization, industrialization, modernization, and immigration.

- The Social Gospel movement attracted liberal Protestants who believed that individual salvation depended on the reform of American society at large. Conservative Protestants, some of whom described themselves as fundamentalists, favored a form of Christianity that remained suspicious of the changing American religious landscape. Tensions between liberal and conservative Protestants reached a high point with the Scopes "Monkey" Trial of 1925.

- As European immigration to the United States continued to rise, Roman Catholics and Jews debated the extent to which they should assimilate to American society. A revival of nativism and xenophobia in the 1920s led to a considerable drop in new immigration to the United States, as well as a reinforcement of ethnic divisions between Protestants, Catholics, and Jews.

- Asian immigrants introduced Buddhism, Hinduism, and other non-Western religions to the United States. Chinese and Japanese communities concentrated in California, where they established temples and addressed the religious needs of their respective adherents. The 1893 World's Parliament of Religions was especially important to the popularization of Buddhism and Hinduism to white Americans, although a series of restrictive immigration laws effectively ended Asian immigration to the United States by the 1910s.

- After a century of forced relocations and social alienation, many Native Americans challenged the American government's vision for Indian life with revitalization and resistance movements. A pan-Indian movement known as the Ghost Dance drew a considerable following during the late nineteenth century, only to be resisted by Christian missionaries and American military forces.

FURTHER READING

For insight into the relationship between religion and race after the Civil War, see William Montgomery, *Under Their Own Vine and Fig Tree: The African American Church in the South, 1865–1900*

(Baton Rouge: Louisiana State University Press, 1993); Edward Blum, *Reforging the White Republic: Race, Religion, and American Nationalism, 1865–1898* (Baton Rouge: Louisiana State University Press, 2007); Paul Harvey, *Freedom's Coming: Religious Culture and the Shaping of the South from the Civil War through the Civil Rights Era* (Chapel Hill: University of North Carolina Press, 2007); Charles Reagan Wilson, *Baptized in Blood: The Religion of the Lost Cause, 1865–1920* (Athens: University of Georgia Press, 1980); Milton Sernett, *Bound for the Promised Land: African American Religion and the Great Migration* (Durham, NC: Duke University Press, 1997); and Anthea Butler, *Women in the Church of God in Christ: Making a Sanctified World* (Chapel Hill: University of North Carolina Press, 2007).

For works on the development of liberal and conservative forms of Protestantism, see Ralph Luker, *The Social Gospel in Black and White: American Racial Reform, 1885–1912* (Chapel Hill: University of North Carolina Press, 1998); Ronald White and C. Howard Hopkins, *Social Gospel: Religion and Reform in Changing America* (Philadelphia: Temple University Press, 1976); Susan Curtis, *A Consuming Faith: The Social Gospel and Modern American Culture* (Baltimore: Johns Hopkins University Press, 1991); William Hutchinson, *The Modernist Impulse in American Protestantism* (Durham, NC: Duke University Press, 1992); Grant Wacker, *Heaven Below: Early Pentecostalism and American Culture* (Cambridge, MA: Harvard University Press, 2003); Matthew Avery Sutton, *Aimee Semple McPherson and the Resurrection of Christian America* (Cambridge, MA: Harvard University Press, 2009); and George Marsden, *Fundamentalism and American Culture*, Second Edition (New York: Oxford University Press, 2006).

Books about the religions of immigrant and native groups include James Fisher, *Communion of Immigrants: A History of Catholics in America* (New York: Oxford University Press, 2007); James O'Toole, *The Faithful: A History of Catholics in America* (Cambridge, MA: Belknap Press of Harvard University Press, 2008); Hasia Diner, *The Jews of the United States* (Berkeley: University of California Press, 2006); John Erickson, *Orthodox Christians in America* (New York: Oxford University Press, 1999); Richard Hughes Seager, *Buddhism in America* (New York: Columbia University Press, 2000); Richard Hughes Seager, *The World's Parliament of Religions:*

The East/West Encounter, Chicago, 1893 (Bloomington: Indiana University Press, 2009); Gregory Evans Dowd, *War under Heaven: Pontiac, the Indian Nations and the British Empire* (Baltimore: Johns Hopkins University Press, 2004); and Gregory Ellis Smoak, *Ghost Dance and Identity: Prophetic Religion and American Indian Ethnogenesis in the Nineteenth Century* (Berkeley: University of California Press, 2008).

6

RELIGIOUS DIVERSITY IN A GLOBALIZING AMERICA, 1920s TO 2010s

The maturation of the United States into a global superpower was matched by the diversification of the American religious landscape during the twentieth century. Change came first with the disruptive consequences of the Great Depression and World War II, as many Christian Americans reconsidered the role of religion in both American society and the global community. It was in the aftermath of these events that Protestants and Catholics found reason to cooperate against the perceived evils of the Soviet Union and within the booming postwar economy. This ecumenical goodwill also applied to Jewish Americans, leading some to describe the 1950s as a decade that witnessed the formation of a Judeo-Christian tradition. Not far beneath the surface, however, was a level of social discontent that formed the basis for the civil rights, feminist, and antiwar movements of the 1960s and 70s. Religious organizations played a critical role in these and other efforts to reform society for African Americans, women, and the poor. Not everyone welcomed these liberal advances, leading to the consolidation of white Christian conservatism into what has come to be called the Religious Right. Adding to the religious entanglements of postwar America was a new phase of immigration that introduced unprecedented numbers of Buddhists, Hindus, Muslims, and non-European Christians to the American populace. Such changes to the country's religious composition have prompted some to regard the United States as a post-Christian or post-Protestant nation, while recognizing that the historical legacy and political potency of

Christianity remains applicable to American life in the twenty-first century.

THE GREAT DEPRESSION AND THE INTERWAR YEARS

Almost everyone reading this book has seen Dorothea Lange's (1895–1965) iconic photograph of the Great Depression, known as "Migrant Mother." Taken in 1936, it captures what Lange described as a "hungry and desperate mother" with "her children huddled around her" under a lean-to tent in Nipomo, California. The woman in the photograph – revealed in 1978 to be Florence Owens Thompson of Modesto, California – was at the time a migrant worker eking out a living just like four million other displaced people who moved from the so-called "Dust Bowl" of the Midwest to the West coast during the 1930s. Although hardly a scholar of religion, or even someone who personally identified with a particular religion, Lange took other pictures of more obviously religious subject matter – church buildings, prayer services, people singing hymns, a Sunday school class, a bus emblazoned with the words "Jesus Saves." In one of the photo captions, she wrote, "Many Texans, Oklahomans, and Arkansans are settling in this country. Their cultures and forms of religious expression are being transferred with them." Like Jacob Riis's (1849–1914) documentary photographs of the urban poor in the 1890s, Lange intended for her images of Depression-era hardship to raise awareness and maybe spur people to action, and this included the occasional gesture to the portability and ordinariness of religion for millions of struggling Americans.

Lange was one among several dozen photographers employed by the U.S. government to document the human cost of the Great Depression. Approximately 164,000 black and white negatives remain of their work in the Library of Congress. The photographs were a small part of a much more comprehensive federal program to end the economic depression of the 1930s. It was called the New Deal. Under the leadership of President Franklin Delano Roosevelt (1882–1945) – a blue-blooded Episcopalian from Hyde Park, New York – the New Deal brought together Protestant, Catholic, and Jewish policymakers to address the social and financial ills of a nation suffering from an unemployment rate that reached almost 25 percent of the adult population. The magnitude of the New Deal's social welfare system was unprecedented in American history. For the first time, the federal government replaced religious organizations, denominations, and churches as the chief provider of social services to America's needy. That being said, the New Deal continued to work hand-in-glove with many charitable wings of religious groups. Such cooperation had a lot to do with what the historian Andrew Preston saw as Roosevelt's ecumenical spirit. "Building on Lincoln's ecumenical civil religion," Preston wrote, "Roosevelt was the first president to prioritize faith itself, as opposed to Protestantism or even Christianity, as the essence of American democracy."

The ecumenical features of Roosevelt's character can be seen in the level of Catholic involvement in the New Deal. Monsignor John A. Ryan (1869–1945), a professor of moral theology and political science at the Catholic University of America, was instrumental in convincing other Catholics to support the New Deal. As a priest who came of age after the release of *Rerum Novarum*, Ryan wrote a dissertation in 1906 entitled "A Living Wage" and later became the director of the Social Action Department of the National Catholic Welfare Council. Ryan's economic progressivism proved influential to fellow Catholics Robert Wager (1877–1953), senator from New York and author of the National Labor Relations Act and Social Security Act; and Philip Murray (1886–1952), president of the United Steelworkers of America and the Congress of Industrial Organizations. Millions of working-class Catholics, while not directly informed by Ryan and other Catholic intellectuals, also supported Roosevelt's New Deal with their political activism, electoral votes, and labor union membership. As just one sign of Roosevelt's attention to his Catholic constituency, 51 of 214 federal judges appointed by Roosevelt were Catholic, compared to just eight Catholics appointed by the previous three presidents.

Two other Catholics – Charles Coughlin (1891–1979) and Dorothy Day (1897–1980) – proved deeply influential public figures during the New Deal era. Coughlin was a priest based in the Detroit area. He was also one of the most recognizable radio personalities of the 1930s, reaching upwards of 30 million listeners a week. He published a nationally circulated newsletter called "Social Justice," a reference to his understanding of the social and economic teachings of *Rerum Novarum*. Although initially supportive of the New Deal, Coughlin retracted his backing as he became more involved with right-wing reactionary groups like the Christian Front. Coughlin was also an anti-Semitic bigot. In a particularly egregious instance, he published a version of the *Protocols of the Elders of Zion*, a grossly anti-Semitic document purporting to prove that Jews were plotting to take over the world. Like Coughlin, Dorothy Day admired the progressive social positions of Pope Leo XIII. In 1933, she founded the Catholic Worker movement and started publishing the newspaper *The Catholic Worker*. While attaining nowhere near the level of Coughlin's notoriety, Day received acclaim for her advocacy for the poor and her criticism of American-style capitalism. She and her fellow Catholic Workers organized "houses of hospitality" for the poor and homeless. And unlike Coughlin, whose influence all but vanished after he publicly supported Nazism and fascism, Day continued to represent a version of Catholicism that was committed to radical activism, nonviolent resistance, and direct action against poverty, racism, and war. Even at the age of 75, Day was arrested for picketing with Cesar Chavez (1927–93) in support of the United Farm Workers.

Protestant reactions to the social and economic disruption of the Great Depression depended on where one fell on the conservative–liberal theological spectrum, as well as on one's luxury to indulge in heady intellectual debates while trying to find a job and feed a family. The Scopes Trial of 1925 was still relatively fresh in the minds of Americans, leaving many white evangelical and fundamentalist Protestants outside the mainstream of national politics. Those with connections to the Social Gospel movement – many of whom came to be known as Mainline Protestants – were now questioning the extent to which modernism was good for Christianity. And African Americans, about a quarter of whom had moved to the urban North during the Great Migration, continued to maneuver themselves in a society still deeply marked by the racist laws of Jim Crow. Add to this mélange of religious perspectives the growing importance of sports, entertainment, and celebrity to popular culture, and it's no wonder that the historian Robert Handy described the 1920s and 1930s as a period of "religious depression."

Several Protestant theologians and ministers provided national audiences with a reappraisal of Christianity in the aftermath of

World War I and in the midst of the Great Depression. Their viewpoints came to be called "neo-orthodoxy," which amounted to a critique of the previous generation's optimistic evaluation of humanity, trust in modern science, and progressive view of the future. Harry Fosdick, the arch-modernist minister himself, even came to question the possibility for reconciling Christianity with the modern age. In a 1935 sermon entitled "The Church Must Go Beyond Modernism," Fosdick argued that "[h]armonizing slips easily into compromising," which could result in Christian adaptations to "contemporary nationalism, contemporary imperialism, contemporary capitalism, contemporary racialism." He concluded, "We cannot harmonize Christ with modern culture. What Christ does to modern culture is to challenge it."

The intellectual foundation of Fosdick's neo-orthodoxy came from the Swiss theologian Karl Barth (1886–1968) and the Danish theologian Søren Kierkegaard (1813–55). Drawing on his Calvinist background, Barth insisted on the incompatibility of the human and the divine, while Kierkegaard took an existentialist position on the individual encounter with God through a state of "fear and trembling." Two German-American brothers from Missouri – Reinhold (1892–1971) and H. Richard (1894–1962) Niebuhr – came to encapsulate the Protestant neo-orthodox posture in twentieth-century America. In his book *Moral Man and Immoral Society* (1932), Reinhold criticized his fellow Protestant theologians for accommodating their Christian beliefs to secular social forces. It was through the individual agent, not the collective whole, that Reinhold hoped for there to be a reinvigoration of social justice in modern society. H. Richard's commentary on American society took a more historical turn in his book *The Kingdom of God in America* (1937), in which he sought to reclaim the Puritan tradition of colonial New England as the basis for a distinctly American form of Christianity that persisted even amidst the religious diversity of the twentieth century.

WORLD WAR II AND THE JUDEO-CHRISTIAN TRADITION

From 1939 to 1945, much of the world was at war. Total casualties were staggering: at least 15 million killed in battle, 25 million wounded in battle, and 45 million dead civilians. Approximately 416,000 American soldiers, sailors, and marines died during the conflict, compared to 2 million Japanese, 4 million Chinese, 5.5 million German, and 10 million Soviet military personnel. Add to these unprecedented death tolls the extermination of around 6 million European Jews by Adolph Hitler's (1889–1945) Nazi regime, and we're left to imagine the religious ramifications of such incredible levels of human suffering and social transformation. Then there was the American home front, where women filled jobs traditionally held by men, while the size of government mushroomed to unprecedented levels as the nation kept a war footing in Europe, Asia, and Africa. In an interview after the war, the Catholic chaplain Father George Zabelka (1915–92) commented that "the whole structure of the secular, religious, and military society told me clearly that ... God was on the side of my country." What about the morality of killing? Zabelka, like most Americans during the war, "was certain that this mass destruction was right, certain to the point that the question of its morality never seriously entered my mind."

Of course, the religious history of American involvement in World War II was far more complicated than Zabelka's commentary on the righteousness of the U.S. military effort. But as chaplain to the 509th Composite Group on Tinian Island in the Pacific Ocean in 1945, Zabelka gained a unique perspective on the cost of war when he blessed the B-29 missions that dropped atomic bombs on the Japanese cities of Hiroshima and Nagasaki. Years later, he would renounce his involvement in the war. "All I can say today is that I was wrong," Zabelka said to an audience commemorating the fortieth anniversary of the bombings. "Christ would not be the instrument to unleash such horror on his people." Paul Fussell (1924–2012), an Army infantry officer who received a bronze star and purple heart for his actions in World War II, held a different opinion about the dropping of the atomic bombs, one that distinguished between those who experienced combat firsthand and those who did not. In an essay for *The New Republic* entitled "Thank God for the Atom Bomb," Fussell, now a distinguished scholar of American literature, dismissed the perspectives of men like Zabelka, because "few of those destined to be blown to pieces if the main Japanese islands had been invaded went on to become our most effective men of letters." Most of the men who experienced combat were, instead, "relatively inarticulate" and "not elaborately educated," and most of them "have remained silent about what they know."

Very little work has been done on the American experience of religion during World War II. Fussell described the war as "a notably secular affair," at least for your average American G.I., despite the fact that approximately ninety-five percent of service members identified themselves as Protestant, Catholic, or Jewish. Writing about the myth of the so-called "Greatest Generation," the historian Kenneth Rose argued that "if there were no atheists in foxholes, it was only because troops were too indifferent to religion to bother becoming atheists." And in a 1947 study entitled *The American Soldier*, the Social Science Research Council noted that "many magical or semi-magical practices have been reported among combat men," including the performance of pre-battle rituals and the carrying of steel-plated pocket bibles and rabbit's feet.

Such everyday, on-the-ground, lived experiences of wartime religion often stood in contrast to the official pronouncements of America's military elite. Speaking before the Serviceman's Christian League in 1944, General Dwight Eisenhower (1890–1969) assured his audience that "the Allied soldier sees himself as a defender of those great precepts of humanitarianism preached by Christ and exemplified in the way of life for which all true democrats stand." With encouragement from politicians and parents on the home front, many senior officers like Eisenhower tried to meet the religious needs of those under their command by fielding a sizeable chaplain corps and supporting the work of religious organizations like the Young Men's Christian Association, the Salvation Army, the National Catholic Community Service, and the Jewish Welfare Board among the troops. The reality, as is usually the case, fell somewhere between the skepticism of Fussell and the boosterism of Eisenhower.

The aftermath of World War II brought many changes to life in the United States. Millions of men returned from years of war in foreign lands to their homes and schools and jobs. Millions more women left their wartime jobs in factories and on farms, resulting in dramatic rises in marriage rates and birth rates throughout the 1940s and 50s. Their children would come to be known as the Baby Boomer generation. Many of these families would move from the cities to the suburbs. African American service members, after experiencing some degree of racial integration in the military, were met with levels of racism that in some cases exceeded the prewar years, effectively setting the stage for advances in the Civil Rights Movement during the 1950s and 60s. And approximately 110,000 Japanese Americans – men, women, and children – were released from internment camps with their traditional family units in disarray. As we will see, religion played a decisive role in the reconfiguration of American society for these and other groups in postwar America.

The Cold War between the United States and the Soviet Union provided Protestants, Catholics, and Jews with a common cause against Communism. Fears reached new highs with the Soviet completion of an atomic bomb (1949), Mao Zedong's Communist revolution in China (1949), and American involvement in the Korean War (1950–3). Catholics in homes, schools, and churches prayed for the conversion of so-called atheistic Communist countries. Also popular among Catholics was devotion to Our Lady of Fatima, a Marian following based on the supposed apparition of the Virgin Mary in Portugal that included an apocalyptic warning against the spread of "the evil doctrines of atheistic Russia." Outspoken Catholic anti-Communists included Francis Cardinal Spellman (1889–1967), who was the Archbishop of New York and Apostolic Vicar for the U.S. Armed Forces during World War II, the Korean War, and the Vietnam War; and Monsignor Fulton Sheen (1895–1979), host of the television show *Life is Worth Living* that reached up to thirty million weekly viewers. Spellman and Sheen, like other members of the clergy, tapped into the patriotic zeal of postwar Catholics by fusing American nationalism with Catholic triumphalism. In the words of the Jesuit theologian John Courtney Murray (1904–67), "it would be almost impossible to set limits to the danger of Communism as a spiritual menace." But by far the most notorious Catholic anti-Communist was Joseph McCarthy (1908–57), the Wisconsin senator who claimed to have a list of State Department officials with ties to the Communist Party in 1950. With support from Spellman and Catholic organizations like the Knights of Columbus and the Catholic War Veterans, McCarthy channeled a brand of American Catholicism that identified the "Red Scare" as an existential threat both to the United States and the Catholic Church.

Widespread opposition to Communism contributed to the reconsolidation of conservative and fundamentalist Protestants in American public life. For the many who held premillennialist views, the global spread of Communism fueled popular representations of how the End Times might come. Still others continued to find ways to connect the Catholic Church to obstacles in the way of American democracy. Paul Blanshard (1892–1980), an atheist writer with a background as a Congregationalist minister, found enthusiastic audiences for his books *American Freedom and Catholic Power* (1949) and *Communism, Democracy and Catholic Power* (1951). In the latter publication, Blanshard drew similarities between the Kremlin and the Catholic Church on subjects like "structure of power," "devices of deification," "thought control," and "management of truth."

The Christian Anti-Communist Crusade was just one of many groups that stemmed from the larger umbrella organization known as the National Association of Evangelicals (NAE). Founded in 1942, the NAE provided so-called "neo-evangelicals" with an alternative ecumenical vehicle to counter the efforts of mainline Protestant denominations to influence American society and government. Speaking to a crowd in Los Angeles in 1949, a young and upcoming preacher affiliated with the NAE had this to say about Communism: "I believe today that the battle is between communism and Christianity! And I believe the only way that we're going to win that battle is for America to turn back to God and back to Christ and back to the Bible at this hour! We need a revival!" The preacher's name was William Franklin Graham (1918-), but he usually went by his nickname, Billy.

Billy Graham's life and career spans a period that saw many evangelical Protestants reasserting themselves into American culture and politics. Born into a Presbyterian family, educated at the fundamentalist Bob Jones College and moderate Wheaton College, and ordained a Baptist minister, Graham's early social and intellectual influences reflected the wide spectrum of evangelical Protestantism in the middle of the twentieth century. Graham's ability to exploit mass media outlets helped broadcast his message of premillennialism, anti-Communism, biblical literalism, and American exceptionalism to national and international audiences. On the realities of racism and segregation, the historian Steven Miller labeled Graham a "racial moderate." Graham refused to speak at segregated revivals as early as 1953, argued that America's record on race relations actually reinforced Communist criticism of American democracy, and insisted that racism existed because of the absence of God in society. In 1957, following the participation of Martin Luther King Jr. (1929–68) in one of Graham's "crusades" at Madison Square Garden, the country's leading civil rights leader told Graham that "you have courageously brought the Christian gospel to bear on the question of race in all of its urgent [sic] dimensions." King also reminded Graham that his "tremendous popularity," "extensive influence," and "powerful message" gave him "an opportunity in the area of human rights above almost any other person that we can point to." Such praise from King did not include Graham's continued association with segregationist ministers and politicians in the South, as well as his Christian justification for American intervention in Vietnam.

A statistical breakdown of religious adherence in the 1950s suggests that there was a kind of revival of religion in postwar America. Approximately 95 percent of citizens identified themselves as "religious," including 68 percent Protestant, 23 percent Catholic, and 4 percent Jewish. It was during this decade that President Eisenhower, with the guidance of Billy Graham, joined a Presbyterian church and became the first president to be baptized while in office. Nevertheless, historian William Lee Miller described Eisenhower as "a very fervent believer in a very vague religion" that came to be called the "Judeo-Christian tradition." Speaking to a Soviet military leader in 1952, Eisenhower explained that "Our government has no sense unless it is founded in a deeply felt religious faith, and I don't care what it is." This apparent vagueness later appeared in Eisenhower's support for including the words "under God" in the American pledge of allegiance and "In God We Trust" on American currency. The Jewish sociologist Will Herberg (1909–77) addressed America's nebulous religious landscape in his book *Protestant, Catholic, Jew* (1955), in which he argued that Protestants, Catholics, and Jews formed a "triple melting pot" that contributed to a state of "religious pluralism" in postwar America. Despite differences between these three religious "denominations," Herberg believed that all Americans shared a "common religion" that he labeled the "American Way of Life."

In retrospect, we see that Herberg was both right and wrong about religion in America during the 1950s. Indeed, there was a ferment of interdenominational cooperation between some Protestants, Catholics, and Jews on matters related to politics and culture. As seen in organizations like the National Conference of Christians and Jews, the predominantly white proponents of this tri-faith alliance tended to deemphasize ethnic and racial differences between and within religious groups, choosing instead to focus on the nationalist ties that bound Americans. Yet even Herberg viewed such Judeo-Christian attitudes toward religious tolerance as somewhat superficial, especially in light of widespread racial discrimination. Little did Herberg know that racism was just the tip of the iceberg when it came to the identity politics of the 1960s and 70s, a transitional period in American history that was defined by the Civil Rights Movement, feminism, the Vietnam War and antiwar protests, new immigration from Latin America and Asia, and the rise of what would come to be called the "Religious Right." It's to these decades of incredible social transformation that we now turn.

SOCIAL DISCONTENT AND RELIGIOUS REFORM

For almost all of American history, it was unfathomable for a Catholic to be elected president of the United States. Alfred Smith (1873–1944), a Catholic and Democratic governor of New York, tried and failed to win the nation's executive office in 1928. Anti-Catholic sentiment had a lot to do with his loss. In Daytona Beach, Florida, the local school board sent notes home to parents warning that "If [Smith] is elected President, you will not be allowed to have or read a Bible." A Baptist minister in Oklahoma City told his congregation that "If you vote for Al Smith you're voting against Christ and you'll all be damned." The Ku Klux Klan, a semi-secret society with an approximate membership of five million in the 1920s, mailed thousands of postcards to New Yorkers after Smith won the state's Democratic Party nomination. The Klan's message was clear: "We now face the darkest hour in American history. In a convention ruled by political Romanism, anti-Christ has won." And in Kansas a little girl asked her mother, "Mama, why don't they kill that bad man Smith that they told us about in Sunday school?"

Fast-forward to 1960, the year John F. Kennedy (1917–63) ran for president. Kennedy was a Catholic and a Democratic senator from Massachusetts. Throughout the campaign, many of those opposed to Kennedy appealed to the anti-Catholic inclinations of some American voters. For example, Norman Vincent Peale (1898–1993), author of the bestseller *The Power of Positive Thinking* (1952), formed Citizens for Religious Freedom as an organization committed to defeating Kennedy. According to Peale's group, "It is inconceivable that a Roman Catholic president would not be under extreme pressure by the hierarchy of his church to accede to its policies with respect to foreign interests." It was this kind of popular anti-Catholicism that persuaded Kennedy to address the issue of his faith before an audience of Protestant ministers in Houston, Texas. He didn't mince words: "I believe in an America where the separation of church and state is absolute." He went on to promise that he would never accept guidance from the pope on matters of national concern, that he would deny public funding for parochial schools, and that he would defend the First Amendment's guarantee of religious liberty. He even referenced Thomas Jefferson's 1786 "Statute for Religious Freedom" as a model of government that didn't discriminate on the basis of religious affiliation. Two months later, Kennedy narrowly defeated Richard Nixon (1913–94), a nominal Quaker, to became the first Catholic elected to the office of President of the United States.

Following the election of Kennedy, Catholics took another step toward the center of American life with the reforms of the Second Vatican Council. From 1962 to 1965, Pope John XXIII (1881–1963) and the world's bishops convened in Rome once a year to discuss ways to renew the Catholic Church in a changing modern world. *Aggiornamento*, translated as "a bringing up to date," was the watchword of the council. The American theologian and Jesuit priest John Courtney Murray – the same person who advised Kennedy on his religion speech in Houston – was instrumental in writing the council's "Declaration on Religious Freedom," which asserted that religious liberty was a civil right sanctioned by God and protected by governments. Another council document conceived of the Catholic Church as "the People of God," in effect empowering the laity to play a more pronounced role in church functions alongside the clergy. But the document that had the most immediate and noticeable impact on everyday Catholics was the "Constitution on Sacred Liturgy," which marked a decisive turn away from the Latin-based Tridentine mass and toward a liturgy spoken in the vernacular that encouraged active lay participation.

While some Catholics opposed the liberalizing effects of Vatican II, others responded to the church's reforms with enthusiasm. For a start, the council's "Pastoral Constitution on the Church in the Modern World" could be interpreted as a revolutionary call to action. "Every type of discrimination," the constitution stated, "whether social or cultural, whether based on sex, race, color, social condition, language or religion, is to be overcome and eradicated as contrary to God's intent." Women religious – nuns and sisters often living in cloistered communities before Vatican II – were quick to adjust their vocations to suit more public roles in schools, hospitals, and other social justice initiatives. Still other laywomen like the scholar Rosemary Radford Ruether (1936-) applied feminist and liberation theologies to their critiques of the Catholic Church and its role in racial and sexist injustices. As a teacher in Howard University's School of Religion during the 1960s, Ruether was deeply influenced by the Civil Rights Movement's campaign for racial equality. It isn't surprising, then, that Ruether's first book *The Church Against Itself* (1967) called for Catholics "to strip away all churchly self-mythology" and to recognize "that there is liberty of conscience within the church itself." The following year, Pope Paul VI (1897–1978) issued the encyclical *Humanae Vitae*, effectively banning Catholics from using birth control and insisting "that each and every marriage act must remain open to the transmission of life." Ruether and other liberal Catholic theologians publicly criticized the church's position on birth control. But it wasn't just theologians who opposed the pope's teaching. Based on a 1970 study, almost eighty percent of Catholic women between the ages of twenty and twenty-four continued to control the size of their families with forms of birth control other than abstinence or the rhythm method.

The responses of Reuther and millions of other American Catholic women to *Humanae Vitae* were, at least in part, a product of the feminist movement of the 1960s. Central to feminism was the unmasking and dismantling of male-dominated institutions. For many women, this meant reimagining their churches and synagogues as non-sexist havens for both men and women to form partnerships in accordance with biblical teachings. Pointing to passages of the kind found in Paul's letter to the Galatians – "There is no such thing as Jew or Greek, slave and freeman, male and female, for you are all one in Christ Jesus" – women in mainline Protestant churches gradually became eligible for ordination as ministers. Catholic nuns, although barred from the priesthood, asserted their role as stewards of the Catholic Church by organizing the Leadership Conference of Women Religious. And Reform Jewish women followed in the footsteps of Sally Priesand (1946-), author of *Judaism and the New Woman* (1975) and the first woman rabbi ordained in the United States in 1972.

Not all feminists aligned with the priorities of reformers like Reuther and Priesand. Some women abandoned hope for reforming the misogyny of their respective religious traditions. Mary Daly (1928–2010), the first woman theologian on the Catholic faculty at Boston College, came to represent a more antagonistic position against religious institutions with a history of patriarchy. Inspired by Simone de Beauvoir's (1908–86) critique of androcentrism in *The Second Sex* (1948), Daly wrote *The Church and the Second Sex* (1968) as an analysis of how "the Christian religion has been an instrument of the oppression of women." In her next book, *Beyond God the Father* (1973), Daly argued for the liberation of sexist theological language, which involved "a *castrating* of language and image that reflect and perpetuate the structures of a sexist world." First and foremost, this required an abandonment of patriarchal terminology associated with "God the Father." With the maturation of feminism in the 1970s and 80s, African American and Latin American women drew distinctions between the feminist experiences of white women and women of color. Alice Walker (1944-), author of the novel *The Color Purple* (1982), coined the term "womanist" to describe black feminism, while Ada Maria Isasi-Diaz (1943–2012) has been called the mother of "mujerista" theology. In both cases, womanist and mujerista theologians incorporated the culturally specific experiences of ethnicity and race into their visions of both humanity and divinity.

The advancement of women's rights coincided with local and national movements to end racism and segregation in the United States. Collectively known as the Civil Rights Movement, many of these efforts flowed from the pews and sanctuaries of African

American churches. At mid-century, about two-thirds of African Americans identified with the Baptist tradition, while the other third went to Methodist churches. Pentecostalism drew an important minority of African American churchgoers, as did Catholicism concentrated in parts of Louisiana and Maryland. From the literary giant James Baldwin (1924–87), who experienced a conversion in one of Harlem's Pentecostal storefront churches as a teenager, to Mahalia Jackson (1911–72), the daughter of a Baptist preacher who was a leading voice in Chicago's gospel music circles – it could be said that almost all African Americans in the twentieth century were somehow influenced by their experiences of Christianity. And it's worth repeating that black women comprised a majority of active church participants, a fact that also translated to marches and protests associated with the Civil Rights Movement.

As we have already seen, the tradition of black protest did not begin in 1954 with the U.S. Supreme Court's decision to desegregate schools in *Brown v. Board of Education of Topeka, Kansas*. But the 1950s did witness unprecedented steps toward racial equality that would reach a high point with the Civil Rights Act of 1964 and a low point with the assassination of Martin Luther King Jr. in 1968. It was at the Holt Street Baptist Church in Montgomery, Alabama, that approximately six thousand black citizens elected King to lead a bus boycott. In a speech that night, King reminded the audience that "we are a Christian people. We believe in the Christian religion. We believe in the teachings of Jesus." Born in Atlanta, Georgia, and with a Ph.D in theology from Boston University, King fused many of the ideas of the white Protestant theologian Reinhold Niebuhr with those of the Indian reformer Mohandas Gandhi (1869–1948), ultimately leading to a Christian concept of justice through nonviolence that came to define much of the Civil Rights Movement.

Of course, King was not the only church leader of the Civil Rights Movement. He and other black ministers founded the Southern Christian Leadership Conference (SCLC) in 1957 as a way to organize churches against white oppression. On the night before the "Good Friday March" on Birmingham, Alabama, in 1963, the Baptist minister Ralph Abernathy (1926–90) reminded the marchers that "Almost 2000 years ago Christ died on the cross for us. Tomorrow we will take it up for our people and die if necessary."

The next day, both Abernathy and King were arrested for participating in an illegal demonstration, along with dozens of other men, women, and children. While in prison, King would pen a "Letter from a Birmingham City Jail" to his fellow clergymen, which included a defense of direct action against unjust laws and a belief that "when these disinherited children of God sat down at lunch counters they were in reality standing up for the best in the American dream and the most sacred values of our Judeo-Christian heritage." Several days later, the segregationist police commissioner Theophilus "Bull" Connor (1897–1973) ordered firemen to use their hoses and policemen to use their dogs against the marchers. News of the violence against peaceful protesters received national media coverage, ultimately forcing Kennedy to intervene on behalf of Birmingham's black community.

In September of 1963, white segregationists perpetrated another horrific act of violence against black citizens of Birmingham. Four girls were killed when a bomb detonated under the steps of the Sixteenth Street Baptist Church before Sunday services. Their names were Addie Mae Collins, Denise McNair, Carole Robertson, and Cynthia Wesley. For many African Americans, the Birmingham church bombing was just one more reminder that King's nonviolent resistance strategy wasn't working. Still others questioned the very legitimacy of Christianity to the lives of African Americans. Writing about her experiences growing up black in Mississippi, Anne Moody (1940–2015) wondered why "God didn't seem to be punishing anyone" for past and present manifestations of white supremacy. Whose side was God on, anyway? "It seemed to me now," Moody wrote in her memoir *Coming of Age in Mississippi* (1968), "that there must be two gods, many gods, or no god at all." The move away from Christian nonviolence received a boost with the formation of the Student Nonviolent Coordinating Committee (SNCC) in 1960. With the guidance of Ella Baker (1903–86), a longtime civil rights activist and critic of King's methods, many SNCC members started to endorse the concept of "Black Power" and the practice of public militancy. As chairman of SNCC, Stokely Carmichael (1941–98) argued that black power was "about bringing this country to its knees any time it messes with the black man." It was about "wag[ing] a psychological battle on the right for black people to define their own terms, define themselves as they see fit, and organize themselves as they see fit," regardless of what powerful white institutions expected of African Americans.

Black Muslims represented another group of African Americans who favored militant protest over nonviolent resistance. As discussed in the previous chapter, the Nation of Islam, under the leadership of Elijah Muhammad, was a black nationalist organization that rejected the authority of "white devils" and believed in the superiority of the black race. The Nation of Islam's place in American public life moved from the margin to the center with the rise in popularity of Malcolm X (1925–65) during the 1960s. Born with the name Malcolm Little in Omaha, Nebraska, Malcolm X would come of age in Harlem, New York, where he worked as a pimp and drug dealer before being arrested for burglary in 1946. He emerged from incarceration as a convert to the Nation of Islam and an effective spokesperson for the "complete separation of the two races." After going on a *hajj* (pilgrimage) to Mecca in 1964, however, Malcolm X left the Nation of Islam, tempered his position on black separatism, and started his own Muslim organization. As told by Alex Haley (1921–92) in *The Autobiography of Malcolm X* (1964), Malcolm X returned from Mecca deeply influenced by Sunni Islam and what he saw as "the color-blindness of the Muslim world's religious society and the color-blindness of the Muslim world's human society." Furthermore, he argued that "Only Islam could keep white Christians at bay" and save African Americans from the racism of white Christianity. In 1965, Malcolm X was assassinated in New York City by members of the Nation of Islam, likely under the direction of Elijah Muhammad.

One issue that civil rights activists like King, Carmichael, and Malcolm X could agree on was the Vietnam War. Malcolm X rightly pointed out that African Americans were far more likely than whites to get drafted and die in the war. In 1967, for example, 64 percent of eligible African Americans were drafted, compared to just 31 percent of eligible whites. And from 1965 to 1966, the casualty rate for blacks was twice as high as whites. Speaking to students at the University of California Berkeley, Carmichael described the Vietnam War as "illegal and immoral," equating the draft of African Americans to the formation of a black mercenary force. He also rejected President Lyndon Johnson's (1908–73) claim that the United States was bringing democracy to Vietnam. "As a black man living in this country," Carmichael said, "I wouldn't fight to give [democracy] to anybody." And King, even after working with the Johnson administration to pass the Civil Rights Act, criticized the U.S. government for its military aggression against North Vietnam. Ever the pacifist, King wrote in the posthumous essay "A Testament of Hope" that "Millions of Americans are coming to see that we are fighting an immoral war that costs nearly thirty billion dollars a year" while "tolerating almost forty million poor [Americans] during an overflowing material abundance."

African American opposition to the injustices of war also energized other Protestants, Catholics, and Jews. As we've already seen, Dorothy Day, founder of the Catholic Worker movement, remained an outspoken critic of American involvement in Vietnam. "We [Americans] are not performing the works of mercy," she said, "but the works of war." Another Catholic Worker named Roger LaPorte (1943–65) set himself on fire in front of the United Nations building in New York in 1965, an act meant to replicate that of a Vietnamese Buddhist monk who did the same two years earlier in Saigon. Rabbi Abraham Heschel (1907–72), himself an active participant in the Civil Rights Movement, joined other Protestants and Catholics in forming the ecumenical organization Clergy and Laity Concerned About Vietnam (CALCAV). In 1967, over two thousand CALCAV members met in Washington, D.C., to stage marches and protests throughout the capital. In a speech to an assembly of CALCAV activists, Heschel prayed, "Thee, our Father in heaven, help us to banish the beast from our hearts, the beast of cruelty, the beast of callousness." The following day, Heschel met with Secretary of Defense Robert McNamara (1916–2009) at the Pentagon to discuss CALCAV's opposition to the Vietnam War. He was joined by William Sloane Coffin (1924–2006), Yale University chaplain; Richard John Neuhaus (1936–2009), Lutheran minister; and Michael Novak (1933-), Catholic chaplain at Stanford University; among others. At one point during the short meeting, Heschel harangued McNamara for his handling of the war. "He poured forth his anguish," Sloane remembered of Heschel's outrage, "his hands gesticulating pathetically."

Little, if anything, was accomplished during the CALCAV meeting with McNamara. But that isn't to say that other grassroots efforts didn't tap into the growing antiwar sentiment throughout the United States. The Catholic priest Philip Berrigan (1923–2002), for example, and three of his friends poured their own blood over the files of Baltimore's selective service draft board, an act meant to symbolize the bloody consequences of war. Several months later, this time joined by Philip's brother (and Jesuit priest) Daniel Berrigan (1921-), the group removed files from another selective service office in Catonsville, Maryland, where they burned the documents in a parking lot with homemade napalm. Other CALCAV leaders organized events for men to turn in their draft cards in protest of the war, while others made their churches into sanctuaries for draft resisters and deserters to avoid arrest. Yet despite such efforts, many people who opposed the Vietnam War on religious grounds still felt a sense of futility. Ray Abrams, a Baptist minister and sociologist at the University of Pennsylvania, was one of those people. In an epilogue to the fortieth anniversary edition of his book *Preachers Present Arms* (1969), Abrams wrote that "Our society is not geared to accept those who take the teachings of Jesus this seriously.... There is no hope that pacifism or resistance to war has any chance of being anything in the social milieu but playing the role of a gadfly to the government."

WHITE CHRISTIAN CONSERVATISM AND THE RELIGIOUS RIGHT

It wasn't easy for many conservative Christians – most of them white evangelical Protestants, along with some white Catholics – to witness the changes that came with the women's rights movement, the Civil Rights Movement, and the antiwar movement. Adding to their anxiety were the claims of radical theologians that America was a post-Christian nation heading down a one-way street to secularism. In 1966, a cover of *Time* magazine even posed the question: "IS GOD DEAD?" In response, many white Christians applied their conservative theological principles to political issues ranging from prayer in public schools to America's foreign policy against the Soviet Union. This ecumenical movement of Christian conservatism came to be called the Religious Right.

Scholars often point to a series of U.S. Supreme Court decisions in the 1960s and 70s as the ideological basis for the Religious

Right. In *Engel v. Vitale* (1962), the justices ruled that the New York State Board of Regents violated the Establishment Clause of the First Amendment ("Congress shall make no law respecting an establishment of religion") for formulating a prayer to be recited in the state's public schools. A year later, in *School District of Abington Township v. Schempp* and *Murray v. Curlett*, the Supreme Court found it unconstitutional for states to pass laws requiring that students read the Bible and say prayers in the classroom. As was often the case, the same people who opposed the Supreme Court's decision to limit school prayer were also those who lamented the racial desegregation ruling of *Brown v. Board of Education of Topeka, Kansas* (1954). The phenomenon of "white flight" – the decision of some white families to move away from racially diverse urban areas to predominantly white suburban neighborhoods – also included the formation of private Christian schools with race-based admission standards. In Holmes County, Mississippi, for example, white student enrollment in public schools dropped from 771 to zero by the end of the 1960s. In 1971, a federal district court ruled in *Green v. Connally* that "segregation academies" should be denied tax-exempt status because of their discriminatory practices. President Richard Nixon, a Republican, supported the decision; prominent evangelical ministers did not. Almost immediately, the South Carolina-based Bob Jones University received warnings from the Internal Revenue Service for its discriminatory policy of not admitting African Americans. It wasn't until 1983, after over a decade of appellate wrangling, that the Supreme Court handed down an 8-to-1 decision against Bob Jones University. And three years after that, President Ronald Reagan (1911–2004) appointed the case's sole dissenter, William Rehnquist (1924–2005), to the position of chief justice of the Supreme Court.

The issue of abortion also contributed to the formation of the Religious Right. Even before the Supreme Court's decision in *Roe v. Wade* (1973) to legalize first trimester abortions, many Catholic organizations expressed dismay at the growing popularity of pro-choice advocacy that came out of the women's rights movement. After the ruling, Catholic anti-abortion groups employed protest tactics that often resembled those of the Civil Rights Movement, including nonviolent demonstrations and disruptive militancy. According to the historian Randall Balmer, initial responses of evangelical Protestants to *Roe v. Wade* fell somewhere between indifference and support. Many considered abortion to be a strictly "Catholic issue," leading delegates of the Southern Baptist Convention to pass resolutions in 1971, 1974, and 1976 that affirmed the legality of abortion in cases of rape, incest, fetal deformity, and the health of the mother. By the end of the 1970s, however, Paul Weyrich (1942–2008), co-founder of the conservative Heritage Foundation, teamed up with evangelical leaders to galvanize opposition to abortion on the political grassroots level. An added boost to the nascent pro-life movement came when the theologian Francis Schaeffer (1912–84) – arguably the intellectual founder of the Religious Right – produced and circulated a film series entitled *Whatever Happened to the Human Race?* which argued that abortion was just the latest and most egregious example of secular humanism's grip on the United States.

The rise of political activism among conservative Christian groups coincided with the presidential administrations of Jimmy Carter (1924-) and Ronald Reagan. Carter, a former Democratic governor of Georgia and "born-again" Baptist, supported racial integration early in his political career and identified both Billy Graham and the Niebuhr brothers as formative influences. Following his presidential election in 1976, many conservative Christians abandoned their support for Carter after he refused to seek a constitutional amendment banning abortion. Still others faulted Carter for signing legislation associated with the Equal Rights Amendment (ERA), which would have augmented the authority of the federal government to guarantee equal rights regardless of one's sex. Phyllis Schlafly (1924-), a middle-class Catholic from St. Louis, Missouri, launched the organization STOP ("Stop Taking Our Privileges") ERA with the support of many of the same women who opposed abortion and the feminist movement. "The women's libbers," she argued, "are radicals who are waging a total assault on the family, on marriage, and on children." While other issues plagued the Carter administration – chief among them internal divisions within the Democratic Party, a bad economy, energy shortages, and the Iran hostage crisis – historians also credit the grassroots political activism of people like Schlafly for Carter's failed reelection bid in 1980.

Bridging the administrations of Carter and Reagan, leaders of the Moral Majority, a political action group founded in 1979, formed a coalition of conservative-minded Protestants (and some Catholics) against the perceived evils of abortion, feminism, gay rights, big government, and an isolationist foreign policy. No one was more influential in the Moral Majority than Jerry Falwell (1933–2007), a Baptist minister based in Lynchburg, Virginia, who reached four million bible-believing viewers on his television show *Old-Time Gospel Hour* every week. According to a 1976 poll, almost a quarter of the American population identified themselves as "born-again" Christians, many of whom were attracted to Falwell's vision of a Christian nation. In a sermon entitled "The Spiritual Renaissance in America," Falwell described the 1960s and 70s as "the dark ages of the twentieth century." But he found hope in the 1980s, a decade marked by "a wave of religious and political and social conservatism that no one can deny and that portends very good things for the future of the United States of America." Reagan, a former Republican governor of California with a background in Hollywood and without an obvious connection to organized religion, built alliances with the Moral Majority and other conservative Christian groups, ultimately leading to his election in 1980 and reelection in 1984. In one of his more famous speeches to the National Association of Evangelicals, Reagan tapped into the Christian nationalism of born-again Americans when he described the Soviet Union as an "evil empire" and the United States as a nation where "the rule of law under God is acknowledged."

A series of high-profile scandals rocked conservative Christian circles during the 1980s. The problem stemmed from the growing popularity and big business of televangelism. Pat Robertson (1930-), Baptist minister and son of a conservative Democratic senator from Virginia, pioneered television ministry in the 1960s with the creation of the Christian Broadcasting Network. Robertson's onscreen personalities included the Pentecostals Jim (1940-) and Tammy Bakker (1942–2007), who would later own and operate the North Carolina-based *Praise the Lord* television network. Based on a passage from the gospel of Luke – "Give, that it may be given unto you" – the Bakkers promoted a "prosperity theology" that promised riches to those who donated money to their ministry. The Bakkers became wildly wealthy, leading journalists to uncover gross financial misconduct and resulting in Jim's imprisonment in 1989. Oral

Roberts (1918–2009), another Pentecostal televangelist who claimed to be a faith healer, announced in 1987 that God was going to "call him home" (kill him) unless viewers contributed eight million dollars to his Oklahoma-based ministry. Roberts successfully raised the money, but media coverage of the incident only exacerbated negative impressions of televangelism's connection to moneymaking. Another scandal broke the following year when Jimmy Swaggart (1935-), a Pentecostal televangelist from Louisiana with an international following, got caught with a prostitute by a rival minister. At the same time that these scandals were hitting the headlines, Robertson used his Christian television enterprise to run for the 1988 Republican presidential nomination on a platform that mirrored that of Falwell's Moral Majority. Vice President George H. W. Bush (1924-) ultimately won the Republican nomination and general election, due in part to the Moral Majority's endorsement of the Episcopalian son of a U.S. senator who announced on the stump that "Jesus Christ is my personal savior." A year later, Falwell disbanded the Moral Majority, proclaiming that "our mission is accomplished" and expressing pride at the organization's ability to "to train, mobilize and electrify the Religious Right."

Of course, most Americans who identified with the Religious Right didn't stop participating in the political process. They celebrated the collapse of the "atheist" Soviet Union in 1991. Billy Graham capitalized on this sentiment the following year when he held a revival in Moscow that attracted around 100,000 people and carried the slogan *Vozrozhdeniye* (translated "rebirth" or "restoration"). Also in 1991, born-again Christians rallied around Bush's decision to expel Saddam Hussein's Iraqi forces from Kuwait, making the country music singer Lee Greenwood's (1942-) song "God Bless the USA" the unofficial anthem of the conflict. When President Bill Clinton (1946-), a born-again Baptist from Arkansas, attempted to lift the ban on homosexual men and women in the military during his first weeks in office, the pro-life activist Randall Terry (1959-) claimed that "this is going to help us mobilize people to take action for the next four years." He was correct, inasmuch as 75 percent of white evangelicals (20 percent of overall voters) helped the Republican Party gain control of both the Senate and House of Representatives in 1994, something that hadn't happened in forty years. The sexual indiscretions of Clinton didn't mute the Religious Right's claim to the moral high ground of American politics, further energizing conservative Christians to pursue control over state and local political offices throughout the country. And in 2000, after eight years of the Clinton administration, 74 percent of white evangelicals helped elect the bible-believing Methodist George W. Bush (1946-) as president of the United States.

NEW IMMIGRATION AND RELIGIOUS PLURALISM

In 1965, President Lyndon Johnson signed into law the Hart-Celler Immigration Bill. At the signing ceremony, Johnson reassured Americans that "This bill we sign today is not a revolutionary bill. It does not affect the lives of millions. It will not restructure the shape of our daily lives." In retrospect, it's safe to say that Johnson was just plain wrong. The law eliminated the national quota system that gave preferential consideration to European countries, which made it much more possible for people from Latin America, Asia, Africa, and the Middle East to make America their home. Since 1965, almost 60 million people have immigrated to the United States, shifting the number of non-Hispanic whites from 84 percent of the total population in 1965 to 62 percent in 2015. Additionally, Gallup polls demonstrate a rise in the number of American citizens who list "Other" (not Protestant, Catholic, or Jewish) as their religious preference – from approximately 3.9 million (2 percent of total population) in 1965 to 8.6 million (4 percent of total population) in 1975. Today, that number has grown to around 19 million people (6 percent of total population) who identify with a religion other than Will Herberg's "big three" religious traditions.

Scholars are fairly unanimous in dismissing the Judeo-Christian paradigm as a useful way to understand America's religious landscape after the 1960s. Most would agree that religious diversity is just a fact of life in a multicultural nation. Even within Christianity, new immigrants from Korea, Vietnam, China, and the Philippines introduced cultural practices to their respective denominations in ways that heightened the global dimensions of religion in America. The American Catholic Church, in particular, experienced a seismic shift in ethnic composition after 1965. Today, more than a quarter of American Catholics were born outside the United States, most of them coming from Mexico, Puerto Rico, Cuba, El Salvador, and the Dominican Republic. It isn't surprising, then, that approximately 34 percent of today's Catholics are Latinos, with the greatest growth occurring in the southern and western regions of the United States. Of Catholics under the age of 25, more than half of them are Latinos. With these kinds of numbers, statisticians predict that a majority of American Catholics will be Latinos by the year 2050.

The liberalization of immigration laws coincided with a rise in Latino political activism. Two Mexican Americans – Cesar Chavez (1927–73) and Dolores Huerta (1930-) – were instrumental in raising the Catholic Church's awareness of the growing Latino population. Together, Chavez and Huerta founded the National Farm Workers Association in 1962 as an organization committed to the rights of Mexican American laborers. Many associated the popular devotion to Our Lady of Guadalupe with what they called *La Causa* ("the Cause"). Also important to the integration of Latinos into the life of the Catholic Church was the priest and theologian Virgilio Elizondo (1935-). The son of Mexican immigrants, Elizondo established the Mexican American Cultural Center in San Antonio in 1972 as a vehicle for championing Mexican forms of Catholic expression within an Americanized institutional church. He also employed the theological concept of *mestizaje* to describe the Latino synthesis of Spanish Catholicism and Native American religions. Although Elizondo admitted in his book *The Future is Mestizo* (1988) that *mestizo* "modes of expression have not always been recognized as legitimate by outsiders," his efforts have nevertheless contributed to a slow shift in the Catholic Church away from a policy of ethnic homogeneity and toward one of multiculturalism.

Since the 1960s, American Buddhism has come to include three general groups: white converts, fourth and fifth generation Asian Americans, and more recent immigrants and refugees. Some polls find that about half of today's self-identified American Buddhists are white. The roots of this growth can be located in the so-called "Zen Boom" of the 1950s and the scholarship of the Zen Buddhist intellectual Daisetz Teitaro Suzuki (1870–1966). Suzuki's message that the "spirit of Buddhism ... is the spirit of all religions and philosophies" was attractive to many religiously curious Americans, including the Catholic monk Thomas Merton (1915–68) and the Beat poet Gary Snyder (1930-). While white Americans were reading novels like Jack Kerouac's (1922–69) *The Dharma Bums* (1958) and visiting an expanding network of Buddhist temples from California to New York, many ethnic Japanese and Chinese Americans attempted to "mainstream" the organizational structures of their respective Buddhist traditions. In 1944, while imprisoned in a Utah internment camp, a group of Japanese Buddhists formed the Buddhist Churches of America. Chinese Americans followed suit in 1964 with the establishment of the Buddhist Association of the United States. These and other institutions provided middle-class, old-line Buddhist ethnic groups with sites of religious expression and avenues for political participation that, in some cases, intentionally mimicked Christian models of denominationalism.

New immigrants and refugees from Asia added a level of diversity to American Buddhism in ways which echoed some of what we've already seen in American Catholicism and Judaism. Horrific wars in southeast Asia forced thousands of refugees to seek asylum in the United States during the 1970s and 80s, including approximately 640,000 Vietnamese (200,000 of whom were Catholic), 180,000 Cambodians, and 70,000 Laotians, among others. One of these refugees was the Vietnamese Buddhist nun Thich Dam Luu (1932–99). Thich founded the Perfect Harmony Temple in San Jose, California, in 1990, which offered Vietnamese language classes to youths and Buddhist chanting and philosophy classes to adults. Vietnamese affiliates of the temple, although primarily associated with the Mahayana Buddhist tradition, were also influenced by the Vietnamese concept of *Tam Giao* (the "Three Religions" of Confucianism, Daoism, and Buddhism). Moreover, with the encouragement of Thich, Buddhists from other sects regularly interacted with the temple's Vietnamese members. Tibetan monks were among the visitors to the temple, where they introduced Tibet's unique form of Buddhism that combines shamanism with monasticism and meditation. Although much smaller in number – approximately 10,000 Tibetan refugees live in the United States today – the outsized popularity of Tibetan Buddhism is largely the consequence of the charisma and philosophy of the fourteenth Dalai Lama (1935-). With bestselling books like *The Art of Happiness* (1998), the Dalai Lama proliferates his ideas about "the common human religion of kindness and compassion" while also raising awareness of China's oppression against the Tibetan people.

After the United Arab Emirates, the United States is the largest destination for immigrants from India. Hinduism has become a noticeable feature of many urban and suburban communities throughout the country, with 2 million Indian Americans now resident (a figure that has grown from 200,000 in 1980). Acts of piety and worship known as *puja* often occur in the domestic sphere, where Hindus build home altars that reflect the cultural uniqueness of their respective Indian roots and American experiences. Concurrently, Indian Americans, many of whom are well-educated professionals, have moved into the public sphere by investing in the construction of Hindu temples, the first of which was consecrated in Pittsburgh, Pennsylvania, in 1977. Today, only India has more Hindu temples than the United States. It has been in Hindu temples that Indians from a variety of language groups and ethnic backgrounds have developed an ecumenical form of Hinduism that capitalizes on the common religious bonds of a people in diaspora.

As was the case with Buddhism, many white Americans experimented with transplanted versions of Hinduism, especially those associated with itinerant gurus who tapped into the countercultural movement of the 1960s and 70s. With the endorsement of the British pop band The Beatles, the guru Maharishi Mahesh Yogi (1918–2008) gained followers after founding the Students International Meditation Society and popularizing techniques associated with what he called "Transcendental Meditation." The International Society for Krishna Consciousness, also known as Hare Krishnas, practice a more devotional (*bhakti*) form of Hinduism that includes the repeated invocation of the god Krishna, food offerings (*prasada*), and other forms of *puja* in communal settings. A community in rural Alachua, Florida, boasts the largest Hare Krishna membership outside of India. The temple is situated on over 100 acres of pastureland and draws many of its members from the nearby University of Florida. Aside from the few who regularly attend the temple's daily meditational and ritual ceremonies, most area residents recognize the Hare Krishnas for their free vegetarian meals on the college campus and their public dancing and chanting of the words *Hare Krishna* (a name for God meaning "the all-attractive one") and *Rama* (another name for God meaning "the reservoir of pleasure"). In 2013, a man desecrated the Alachua temple with bleach while claiming that the space was "unclean," an act that many interpreted as a hate crime perpetrated against a minority religious group.

Around 3 million Muslims reside in the United States today. That's up from approximately 200,000 Muslim Americans in 1950, but still shy of the number of American Jews in the twenty-first century. A combination of factors contributed to this uptick in the American Muslim population, including the liberalization of American immigration laws, political unrest in several Muslim-majority countries, and job opportunities in the American economy. Uniting most Muslim Americans is Sunni Islam, which isn't surprising considering the fact that around 90 percent of the world's Muslims are Sunni. Shia Muslims in the United States typically have roots in Iran, Iraq, Pakistan, and India. The division between Sunni and Shia Islam goes back to a dispute over the succession of authority after the death of the prophet Muhammad in 632 CE.

With so many Muslims coming from so many parts of the world, ethnic and racial differences also play a role in the diversity of American Islam. That being said, scholars point to five basic tenets of Muslim religious law (*sharia*) that most Muslim Americans follow to some extent. Sometimes called the "Five Pillars of Islam," they include the *shahada* (the core testimony of the Muslim faith that states that there is only one God and the prophet Muhammad is God's messenger); *salat* (ritual prayer performed five times a day while facing Mecca); *zakat* (almsgiving and support for those in need); *sawn* (fasting during the holy month of Ramadan); and *hajj* (the obligation to go on a pilgrimage to Mecca if financially feasible).

Prior to this section of the book, our only encounters with Islam have been in the contexts of African slavery and the Nation of Islam. This is due largely to the fact that so few Muslims immigrated to the United States prior to the 1960s. Syrian-Lebanese immigrants started to settle in the upper Midwest around 1900, ultimately leading to the construction of one of America's first mosques in the small farming town of Ross, North Dakota. In 1952, Muslim Americans from around the country convened in Cedar Rapids, Iowa, to discuss ways to support the growing Muslim American population and to establish the Federation of Islamic Associations of the United States and Canada. This was followed by a series of national events that exposed Muslim Americans to the wider public. In 1957, President Eisenhower cited America's "strong bond of friendship with Islamic nations" when he attended the dedication ceremony of the Islamic Center of Washington, D.C. In 1962, a federal district court decided in the case of *Fulwood v. Clemmer* that Islam was a constitutionally protected religion alongside the "theistic" traditions of Protestantism, Catholicism, and Judaism. And in 1963, international students at the University of Illinois formed the Muslim Student Association (MSA). MSA chapters quickly expanded to other colleges and universities with a mission to welcome new Muslim students into American life. Over time, some MSA members shifted their attention to shaping Muslim American identity on a national level and contributing to the formation of the Islamic Society of North America in 1981.

With such a large population, it isn't surprising that Muslim Americans live all over the United States. But since the early twentieth century, the city of Detroit has been one of the most common destinations for Muslim immigrants, due in part to the Ford Motor Company's openness to employing Muslim Americans as early as the 1910s. Sunni and Shia Muslims, even within the same ethnic group, didn't always see eye-to-eye on how to navigate through American society. Some supported a form of pan-Islamism that would provide both Sunni and Shia Muslims with religious support and social services otherwise unavailable to minority groups. Others believed that two mosques, Sunni and Shia, were better than one. Regardless of this tension between what the historian Sally Howell described as "the *ideal* of the unified Muslim umma [the greater Islamic community] and the reality of a highly diverse Muslim community," Muslims of Detroit interacted with one another on a daily basis at work, grocery stores, schools, and other venues. In 1949, for example, a Muslim youth organization at a mosque in the city of Dearborn (a suburb of Detroit) invited the "children of Islam" to "a party featuring Arabic music and American dances." Organizers hoped that the gathering would function as a sign of Muslim unity to outsiders, because "[s]eparation from each other will do nothing but degrade the status and name of Arabs and Muslims." During the 1970s and 80s, large numbers of Lebanese and Iraqi refugees fled conflicts in their respective countries, making the Detroit area the largest Shia Muslim community in the United States with approximately 75,000 members. More recently, Muslim immigrants from Yemen, Bangladesh, and Bosnia have made Hamtramck, Michigan (also a suburb of Detroit), into the first American city with a majority Muslim population. Once known as "Little Warsaw" for its sizable Polish Catholic community, residents of Hamtramck can now hear the five daily calls to prayer from mosque loudspeakers. For supporters (including some non-Muslims), the public prayers have become a normal feature of the urban soundscape, akin to the ringing of church bells and a sign of America's religious pluralism. For opponents, it's a reminder of the cultural changes that come with religious diversity and the tenuous relationship between new immigrant groups and established residents throughout the United States.

Although Muslims in America represent over seventy ethnic and national backgrounds, we can make some generalizations about the everyday practice of Islam. Practicing Muslims perform the five daily prayers (*salat*) as a way to focus on God (*Allah*) through the recitation of verses found in the Qur'an. In some communities, it's possible to hear the public call to prayer (*adhan*) coming from the voice of a *muezzin* (the man who gives the call to prayer) at a local mosque (*masjid*). Friday prayer (*jum'ah*) is a time for Muslims to gather as a congregation. Those who participate in *jum'ah* listen to sermons from an *imam* (prayer leader) and take time for personal prayer (*du'a*). During the ninth month of the Islamic lunar calendar (*Ramadan*), Muslims abstain from eating, drinking, and sexual activity from dawn to dusk. Everyone over the age of seven is expected to observe the fast. In Minneapolis – home to over 150,000 Muslims, most of them Somali Americans – a youth soccer coach admitted that Ramadan "could be hard on these kids." Breaking the fast is often a festive affair, when families and friends come together around the table to celebrate their kinship and praise Allah. The end of Ramadan is marked by *Eid al-Fitr* (the Festival of Fast-breaking). Some observances of Eid al-Fitr can become quite large. In Houston, for example, around 20,000 area Muslims gather at the George R. Brown Convention Center as a public demonstration of their Muslim identity. As one participant in the annual event told a news reporter, "Basically you could say it's like our Christmas – the Islamic Christmas."

Of course, the comparison between Eid al-Fitr and Christmas is grossly inaccurate. But it says something about efforts on the part of some Muslim Americans to communicate their religious identity to a wider (mostly Christian) public in an age marked by the events of September 11, 2001. The inclination of some people to judge Muslim Americans on the actions of Muslims in other parts of the world has fueled Islamophobia and racial profiling throughout the United States. Annual hate crimes against Muslim Americans are almost five times higher than they were before al-Qaeda operatives hijacked four jetliners, executed attacks against the World Trade Center and the Pentagon, and killed 2,996 civilians. Groups like the Islamic Society of North America (ISNA) have encouraged members "to be mosques without walls" as a way to promote interfaith cooperation and cross-cultural understanding. Ingrid Mattson (1963-) – a Canadian-born convert to Islam (she grew up Catholic), professor of Islamic studies, and former president of ISNA – has been a leader in this regard, having advised the White House and the Department of Homeland Security on faith-based initiatives. Among other things, Mattson has educated the American public on the practice of *hijab* (women covering their body in public) and encouraged Muslim Americans to unite with Christians and Jews around "an axis of goodness and justice."

Muslim Americans represent one among many minority religious groups that have contributed to the diversification of religion in the United States during the twentieth and twenty-first centuries. When we combine the effects of new immigration with the diversity that already exists within Christianity, it's appropriate for us to view the United States as a country without a clear religious center. And while we have already seen how some Americans have reacted to this state of affairs with fear, anger, and activism, others have welcomed the decentering results of globalization and promoted what has come to be called "religious pluralism." It is to the ongoing debate over American religious pluralism that we conclude this book.

SUMMARY

- The national emergencies of the Great Depression and World War II brought Protestants, Catholics, and Jews together like never before in American history. Though theological and ethnic differences remained important, efforts to address domestic and international crises generated opportunities for ecumenical cooperation among many white Americans.

- Social discontent, especially among African Americans and women, formed the basis of the civil rights, feminist, and anti-war movements of the 1960s and 70s. Many reformers applied their religious views to questions of racial, economic, and gender inequalities.

- Evangelical Protestantism experienced a resurgence after World War II and during the Cold War. In reaction to some of the social reforms of the 1960s and 70s, many white evangelical Protestants increased their involvement in American politics as a way to blunt what they perceived as un-American and un-Christian trends in the United States.

- The liberalization of immigration laws in the 1960s added to the religious and ethnic diversity of the United States. Buddhists, Hindus, Muslims, and non-European Christians changed the religious composition of the United States in dramatic ways, leading some to welcome and others to lament the rise of religious pluralism.

FURTHER READING

For books about the role of religion in the Great Depression, World War II, and the Cold War, see Colleen McDannell, *Picturing Faith: Photography and the Great Depression* (New Haven, CT: Yale University Press, 2004); Alison Collis Greene, *No Depression in Heaven: The Great Depression, the New Deal, and the Transformation of Religion in the Delta* (New York: Oxford University Press, 2015); Kenneth Heineman, *The Catholic New Deal: Religion and Reform in Depression Pittsburgh* (University Park: Pennsylvania State University Press, 1999); Michael Snape, *God and Uncle Sam: Religion and America's Armed Forces in World War II* (Rochester, NY: Boydell Press, 2015); Kevin Schultz, *Tri-Faith America: How Catholics and Jews Held Postwar America to Its Protestant Promise* (New York: Oxford University Press, 2011); Jonathan Herzog, *The Spiritual-Industrial Complex: America's Religious Battle against Communism in the Early Cold War* (New York: Oxford University Press, 2011);

and William Inboden, *Religion and American Foreign Policy, 1945–1960: The Soul of Containment* (New York: Cambridge University Press, 2010).

For works related to religious and social reforms of the twentieth century, see James Fisher, *The Catholic Counterculture in America, 1933–1962* (Chapel Hill: University of North Carolina Press, 1989); Mark Massa, *The American Catholic Revolution: How the '60s Changed the Church Forever* (New York: Oxford University Press, 2010); Thomas Carty, *A Catholic in the White House? Religion, Politics, and John F. Kennedy's Presidential Campaign* (New York: Palgrave Macmillan, 2004); Mary Henold, *Catholic and Feminist: The Surprising History of the American Catholic Feminist Movement* (Chapel Hill: University of North Carolina Press, 2008); David Chappell, *Stone of Hope: Prophetic Religion and the Death of Jim Crow* (Chapel Hill: University of North Carolina Press, 2004); Aldon Morris, *The Origin of the Civil Rights Movement: Black Communities Organizing for Change* (New York: Free Press, 1986); and Robert Dannin, *Black Pilgrimage to Islam* (New York: Oxford University Press, 2002).

Discussions of liberal Protestantism and the rise of the Religious Right include the following: David Hollinger, *After Cloven Tongues of Fire: Protestant Liberalism in Modern American History* (Princeton, NJ: Princeton University Press, 2013); Neil Young, *We Gather Together: The Religious Right and the Problem of Interfaith Politics* (New York: Oxford University Press, 2015); Daniel Williams, *God's Own Party: The Making of the Christian Right* (New York: Oxford University Press, 2010); and Randall Balmer, *The Making of Evangelicalism: From Revivalism to Politics and Beyond* (Waco, TX: Baylor University Press, 2010).

The subject of religion and new immigration is covered in Timothy Matovina, *Latino Catholicism: Transformation in America's Largest Church* (Princeton, NJ: Princeton University Press, 2012); Lois Ann Lorentzen et al., *Religion at the Corner of Bliss and Nirvana: Politics, Identity, and Faith in New Migrant Communities* (Durham, NC: Duke University Press, 2009); Kambiz GhaneaBassiri, *A History of Islam in America: From the New World to the New World Order* (New York: Cambridge University Press, 2010); and Sally Howell, *Old Islam in Detroit: Rediscovering the Muslim American Past* (New York: Oxford University Press, 2014).

CONCLUSION

On September 23, 2001, around twenty thousand people packed Yankee Stadium in the Bronx, New York, to participate in what was billed as a "Prayer for America." They were there to reflect upon the events of September 11, 2001. The ceremony opened with a choir singing "Battle Hymn of the Republic," followed by over two hours of prayers and commentary from religious leaders, politicians, celebrities, and other New York dignitaries. Oprah Winfrey (1954-), the master of ceremonies, announced that "we pray today that from the ashes ... will rise a new spirit of beauty and unity in our country, creating a new tapestry of one heart, one hope, one voice, one America." The actor James Earl Jones (1931-) reminded everyone that "our nation is a symbol of liberty, equal opportunity, democracy and diversity. This attack was an attempt to undermine these four pillars of our civic faith." Officers of the New York City Police Department sang the national anthem. The Catholic archbishop of New York gave the invocation. A Jewish rabbi blew a shofar, while another rabbi blessed President George W. Bush for "sound[ing] the clarion call to battle the terrorists at home and abroad and unify the nation to defend freedom, democracy, and, yes, the civilized world." The Spanish tenor Plácido Domingo (1941-) sang "Ave Maria." Rudy Giuliani (1944-), mayor of New York City, welcomed "religious leaders from every faith" to the ceremony, pointing to the Latin motto, *E pluribus unum* ("Out of many, one") as proof that "we find strength in our diversity." Catholic laypeople read from the New Testament in Spanish and English. The Catholic bishop of Brooklyn asked, "Mary queen of peace, pray for us." A representative from a local Sikh temple chanted a prayer. The Boys and Girls Choir of Harlem sang "We Shall Overcome." George Pataki (1945-), governor of New York, imagined that those who died in the terrorist attacks were "looking down" from heaven with pride at "the Muslim deli owners and cab drivers who proudly wave the American flag from their cars and shop windows." A muezzin sang the Islamic call to prayer and an imam ended his remarks with the statement, "We are Muslims, but we are Americans." Bette Midler (1945-) sang her popular song "Wind Beneath My Wings." Representatives from Protestant organizations included the Episcopal bishop of New York, the pastor of New York's Riverside Church, the pastor of New York's Abyssinian Baptist Church, and a district president of the Lutheran Church. The country singer Lee Greenwood sang "God Bless the USA," setting off chants of "USA! USA!" throughout the stadium. The archbishop of the Greek Orthodox Church of America gave the benediction. The last speaker was the leader of a Hindu temple in Brooklyn. "We must stand together," he said, "for remember these final words: A nation's power lies only in the strength of unity. God bless you all!" And with that, the singer Marc Anthony (1968-) took the stage and ended the ceremony with a rendition of "America the Beautiful."

If the post-9/11 "Prayer for America" ceremony isn't an example of American civil religion, then I don't know what is. Following the memorial service, CNN correspondent Martin Savidge observed, "I was struck by really two words that may seem very much opposed to each other … those words are diversity and unity." Indeed, the ceremony was quite intentionally orchestrated to showcase the power of nationalism to unify people from diverse religious back-grounds at a time of tragedy. But as we all know, in the days, months, and years that followed, the unity displayed in Yankee Stadium was met by the corrosive realities of foreign wars, domestic politics, and religious differences. This tension between diversity and unity comes up again and again in historical surveys of religion in America. Some scholars have highlighted the unifying qualities of America's religions by employing the phrase "religious pluralism" to describe the current and future state of the American religious landscape. Others have grown suspicious of the term, if only because conflict within and between religious groups remains such a hallmark of life in the United States. Regardless of where scholars stand on the issue, it's necessary for all of us to think about how Americans negotiate their religious differences in all kinds of contexts, from the public sphere to the private household and from traditional media outlets like Fox News to social media platforms like Facebook.

RELIGIOUS PLURALISM RECONSIDERED

My narrative of religion in America has emphasized diversity more than unity. I go back to Tocqueville's observation in 1835 that the "sects that exist in the United States are innumerable." Of course, when Tocqueville referred to "sects," he was mainly speaking of Christian groups. As we've seen, some of these Christian organizations gained substantial levels of political and cultural clout, perhaps none more powerful than evangelical forms of Protestantism in the nineteenth century. Yet even in the midst of an apparent "Protestant moral establishment," alternative versions of Christianity like Catholicism and Mormonism challenged claims of Protestant orthodoxy and authority. With so many people falling under the category of "Christianity," I've tried to follow the advice of historians like Catherine Brekus and W. Clark Gilpin to think about people in the United States "embroiled in a long, sometimes fractious debate about the possibilities for being appropriately both Christian and American."

In addition to exploring the array of denominational affiliations among Christians, we've seen how other cultural, social, and economic factors influenced the religious identification of people from the colonial period to the present. Chief among differentiating factors were race, ethnicity, gender, and class. The Christianity of a slaveholder in Louisiana was different from that of a Kongolese slave. The Catholicism of a first-generation Polish family living in the city of Chicago hardly matched that of a fourth-generation Irish family living on a farm in Nebraska. The experiences of a female preacher in a backwoods Baptist church didn't mirror that of a male preacher in exactly the same church. And impoverished people who relied on the charity of Christian relief organizations conceived of their place in the world far differently from those with the resources to give to charity. To grasp such variety, the scholar Robert Orsi reminds us of how religious beliefs and practices "have meaning only in relation to other cultural forms and in relation to the life experiences and actual circumstances of the people using them." In other words, context matters when we're trying to understand how Americans have lived their religions alongside other Americans with different religions.

The immigration of non-Christian groups to the United States, especially after 1965, only added to the overall religious diversity of the American religious landscape. As the scholar Stephen Prothero put it, religious diversity is no longer "a proposition to be proved," but "an undeniable fact." Today, as it was in the past, conflicts between religious groups are a common feature of American life. But while some Americans feel threatened, others welcome the opportunity for cultural interaction with people from different religious backgrounds. Efforts to nurture inter-religious exchanges are many. Among academic institutions, the Pluralism Project at Harvard University works "to help Americans engage with the realities of religious diversity through research, outreach, and the active dissemination of resources" to popular audiences. The guiding principles of the Pluralism Project come from its founder Diana Eck, a scholar of comparative religion and advocate for interfaith alliances. For Eck and other contributors to the project, religious pluralism isn't synonymous with religious diversity, and it isn't as simple as tolerating people unlike oneself. Rather, pluralism requires a willful, dialogical, and constructive engagement with diversity that respects differences while allowing for common understanding. Based on the First Amendment's promise of religious freedom, proponents of religious pluralism are trying to make an ideal become a reality, both on the national level and in local communities.

As pluralism has become a kind of civic virtue, some scholars point to recent polls conducted by the Pew Research Center for insight into the extent to which Americans have embraced the doctrines of religious pluralism. In its highly publicized "Religious Landscape Study," Pew found that the number of Christian adherents (Protestants and Catholics) fell from 78.4 percent of U.S. adults in 2007 to 70.6 percent in 2014. Correspondingly, the number of atheists, agnostics, and those who say their religion is "nothing in particular" rose from 16.1 percent in 2007 to 22.8 percent in 2014. To put this into some perspective, those unaffiliated with a specific religious tradition (sometimes called the religious "nones" or the "spiritual-but-not-religious") now outnumber Roman Catholics and are expected to surpass evangelical Protestants in the next decade. During the same period, those who identify with non-Christian religions (mostly Muslims, Buddhists, and Hindus) only grew from 4.7 percent to 5.9 percent. What are we supposed to make of these statistics? Some have argued that the drop in Christian adherence and spike in religious disaffiliation create an atmosphere more conducive to religious pluralism. Others point out that these same trends fuel conflicts both within and between religious groups, Christian and non-Christian. Suffice it to say that the jury is still out.

In the meantime, many scholars have stopped trying to gauge, much less promote, the level of religious pluralism in the United States. Instead, they're interested in how religious pluralism, described by the historian William Hutchinson as a "work in progress," means different things to different people for different reasons in different places at different times throughout the United States. According to the historian Amanda Porterfield, religious pluralism "is not only an idealized way of conceptualizing religion;" it is also an "interpretive framework for tracing the accommodation of diversity in American religious history." Recalling our discussion in Chapter 2 on the history and memory of religion in America, the historian Sydney Ahlstrom blazed a path toward this kind of analysis when he claimed that post-1960s America was a "post-Protestant era," leading the next generation of scholars to highlight diversity as well as unity. Fast-forward to the twenty-first century, and we have scholars like Courtney Bender and Pamela Klassen talking about religion in America "after pluralism." From this perspective, scholars are exploring how people understand religious differences "after pluralism has become a widely recognized social ideal embedded in a range of political, civic, and cultural institutions." Some, like those who identify with the Religious Right, aren't satisfied with the doctrines of religious pluralism and imagine returning America to a Christian monoculture. Others, like the many religious seekers that came of age during the countercultural years of the 1960s, relish the pluralistic turn in American society and look forward to its continued acceptance as a model for living with others. In the human gulf that separates these two poles, we see all kinds of ways in which people live their religions in a fuzzy zone marked by both religious inclusivity and exclusivity.

The Internet is one of these fuzzy zones. In a memo circulated among executives at Microsoft in 1995, Bill Gates (1955-) claimed that "the Internet is a tidal wave" that "changes all the rules" of communication. Since then, we've seen the Internet move from modem-enabled desktop computers to portable wireless devices, and from a relatively static interface for "surfing" a web of information to a highly dynamic platform for social interaction. If the fifteenth-century invention of the printing press democratized the dissemination and interpretation of religious texts during the Protestant Reformation, then the decentralized architecture of the World Wide Web does similar democratizing work on traditional religious institutions but on a much larger and uncontrollable scale. Some scholars have speculated that many of the so-called "religious nones" maintain a religious presence on the Internet, a cyberspace rooted in an ethic of individual expression and self-discovery. And yet people who identify with specific religious traditions also operate in the virtual domain of the Internet, supporting the possibility for both religious pluralism and religious intolerance. The Spanish philosopher Jesus Martín-Barbero (1937-) had something to say about this apparent contradiction, arguing that "despite all the promise of modernity to make religion disappear, what has really happened is that religion has modernized itself." As evidence of this phenomenon, search "#religion" on Twitter and scroll through the results on your iPhone.

MORE QUESTIONS THAN ANSWERS

That about does it for our romp through American religious history. As much as I've been able to cover, no single narrative can ever satisfy our need to know more and to think differently about the place of religion in American life. I'm convinced that I could write an entire chapter apologizing for all of the matters that I failed to report, but then I might feel compelled to scrap the book that you've just completed and produce an entirely new one. That being said, my goal for this book has always been to provide readers with a basic introduction to American religions. This has included both an historical survey of the American religious landscape and a critical reflection on the ways in which scholars approach the study of religion in America. As someone who now knows more than most about American religions, you're in a position to continue exploring the religious features of the United States with your own questions in mind and from your own informed perspective.

FURTHER READING

For books about American religious pluralism, see Courtney Bender and Pamela Klassen, eds., *After Pluralism: Reimagining Religious Engagement* (New York: Columbia University Press, 2010); Diana Eck, *A New Religious America: How a "Christian Country" Has Become the World's Most Religiously Diverse Nation* (San Francisco, CA: HarperSanFrancisco, 2002); William Hutchison, *Religious Pluralism in America: The Contentious History of a Founding Ideal* (New Haven, CT: Yale University Press, 2004); Charles Lippy, *Pluralism Comes of Age: American Religious Culture in the Twentieth Century* (Armonk, NY: M.E. Sharpe, 2000); Charles Cohen and Ronald Numbers, eds., *Gods in America: Religious Pluralism in the United States* (New York: Oxford University Press, 2013); and Catherine Brekus and W. Clark Gilpin, eds., *American Christianities: A History of Dominance and Diversity* (Chapel Hill: University of North Carolina Press, 2011).

INDEX